William Prentice ◀ **KW-328-652** ......p from early childhood, and most of his close relatives either owned or worked for small businesses. Much of his own career followed a different path and, after graduating as a chemist, he spent nearly thirty years in the international oil industry. In the 1970s he left to start his own business as a management consultant and freelance writer. He died in 1984.

Malcolm Bird is the development manager of a major international insurance organization centred in the City of London. He has over twenty years' business experience, in the UK and overseas, with American and British companies. His work has been in the fields of Organization and Methods, computers and general business consultancy.

Also by William Prentice

How to Start a Successful Business

WILLIAM PRENTICE
And
MALCOLM BIRD

How to Make
<u>More</u> Money From
Your Business

GRAFTON BOOKS

A Division of the Collins Publishing Group

LONDON GLASGOW
TORONTO SYDNEY AUCKLAND

Grafton Books
A Division of the Collins Publishing Group
8 Grafton Street, London W1X 3LA

A Grafton Paperback Original 1986

ISBN 0-586-06474-5

Printed and bound in Great Britain by
Collins, Glasgow

Set in Times

Preface

This book has at least one unusual feature. The two joint authors have never met.

Bill Prentice had planned this book and written about half of it when he tragically died. However, Bill was a man who practised what he preached and he had prepared comprehensive notes on his ideas and intentions for the book. This has enabled me to 'pick up the ball' and continue running with it in the direction Bill intended. I have carefully followed Bill's 'directions' and apart from adding my own experience to the detail in the later chapters I suggest that any credit due should go to Bill.

Like Bill I do not claim to be an expert in every possible field of business (if I were I would be as rich as Croesus) and, like him, must exhort you to take competent professional advice on specialist areas such as tax, pensions and legal matters.

Malcolm Bird

Contents

8 *Contents*

Foreword

During the first few months or years of starting a business, the main concern is simply one of survival, of keeping the struggling business alive. It is difficult for the owner to find time to think at this stage. Indeed it may seem hardly necessary to think, since what needs to be done is usually so obvious; the problem is essentially one of priorities.

Not all new businesses survive, alas, but those which do reach a stage when the owner can at last feel that he has proved it is viable. Now be begins to wonder, 'How can I make it more profitable?' The measures needed to achieve this will of course differ greatly, depending upon the nature of the business, the talents of the entrepreneur and his reasons for starting the business.

Nevertheless, there is a method which can be applied to any new business. This book is designed to help the entrepreneur apply this method to his or her own particular business. The reader is taken systematically through the steps: (1) taking stock of where the business stands at present; (2) how to increase income; (3) how to reduce expenditure; (4) how to use money more efficiently.

These steps will highlight the strengths of the existing business, strengths which can be used to make the business grow. The steps will also reveal weaknesses which must be put right to overcome present troubles or prevent future ones. The knowledge about your business gathered in this way is converted into specific advice in a concluding section: (5) How to make it happen in *your* business.

This is designed as a working book and at the end of each chapter certain 'homework' is suggested. By doing this homework, you will build up a survey of the key aspects of your business as you progress through the book. In the concluding chapters you will be shown how to interpret your calculations and comments and turn them into practical measures you can take to make *your* business more profitable. If you follow the method given in this book you will in effect have conducted a DIY management consultancy study, just as an outside consultant might do it, but at much less cost. Moreover, because you have done it yourself, you are much more likely to believe the conclusions and put them into practice.

As the examples in the text show, I am well aware that many new businesses are started by women and some of these become very profitable indeed. Consequently, although I have used 'he', 'him' or 'his' in places to avoid clumsy writing, these should be read as 'she' or 'her' when appropriate.

While every care has been taken to get the facts right, I don't claim to be free from error. Moreover, what is good advice for one business may be inappropriate for another. Consequently, I can accept no legal liability for advice given in this book. You must always check with your own professional advisers that the advice is valid for your business.

PART 1
Where Are You Now?

CHAPTER 1

Pause for Breath

This book is written for people who believe that the business they started a few months – or years – ago is a 'runner'. They have lost the fear that collapse is just around the corner, although they may still get some bad moments. Now they want to increase the return they are getting for the effort they have put in. In short, they want to increase the profitability of their business.

In the next three chapters, we shall delve into the figure side of your business to pinpoint where you stand on a quantitative basis. But before doing so, I want you to sit back and take a more detached, almost philosophical, view. You will probably not be able to answer all the questions off the cuff. In fact, I'd rather you didn't try. If a question doesn't trigger an immediate response, leave it for the time being. The answer will probably come to you later on.

One purpose of this chapter is to start you thinking about the kind of business you really want to be running in the future. You may find that your views have changed since you started the business.

The other purpose of this chapter is to extract as much benefit as possible from your experience to date, however limited that may be, and regardless of whether the experience was pleasant or unpleasant. In fact, you can often learn more from the unpleasant experiences, provided you are willing to be rigorously honest with yourself and recognize where you went wrong.

Some of the topics raised may evoke an intuitive response or 'hunch'. Don't disparage these hunches; a lot more decisions are based on hunches than the business schools like to admit. In the real world, the successful businessman makes many hunch decisions, but only when facts are *not* available. Nor is he afraid to conduct a post-mortem on the unsuccessful ones.

What type of business

Broadly speaking, there are three main types of business activity: making things, selling things, and providing a service. In practice, the boundaries between these may be hard to draw and many businesses display elements of all three. After all, the manufacturer has to sell what he makes and the salesman has to provide some form of service. Nevertheless, in most businesses – and particularly in small businesses – one type is clearly the main activity. What type of business are you running?

Before answering this question, read the following 'cautionary tale':

> Joe's previous business folded up like many others in 1980. He had a modest pension from his earlier employment so in choosing a new business he looked for pleasure as much as income. He had been a stamp collector for many years and decided upon mail-order stamp dealing, operating from his home to minimize overheads. Once under way, he was gratified by the number of customers who commented on the good service he gave. At the same time, he became increasingly resentful of the amount of time he had to spend on rearranging stock and sending out revised lists of offers. It gradually dawned on him that he was running a service business, not a selling business.

Why start a business?

In the example quoted above, Joe started his stamp-dealing business for fun as much as for money. Other people start businesses for many different reasons. Some believe they can make more money working for themselves than for someone else. Some have an idea for a product or service which they are convinced will make their fortune – and occasionally they are right. Some are frustrated, working in a badly run business which they think they could run much better. Some who are unemployed start a business in a mood of desperation, because they cannot get a job. Some are just bored by many years of doing the same job and want to try their hand at something new.

Although money is a powerful spur in many cases, it is not always the main factor. The common theme which comes through almost every entrepreneur's tale of why he started a business is a *desire for independence* – freedom to do his own thing, make his own mistakes, try out his own ideas and reap the rewards – and penalties – of being his own boss.

Why did you start *your* business? To what extent do you think you are achieving your objectives? If you continue running it along present lines and improve its profitability, will the business give you what you want? If you are becoming disenchanted with the business, is this because your wants have altered? Do you now suspect that you may have exchanged one rat race for another? Do you still have the same wants but feel you may have chosen the wrong business? Why did you choose this particular business in the first place?

Problems – and Opportunities!

As you progress through the book, I shall help you examine your business in detail to find out its strengths and weaknesses. I shall also discuss many ways in which these strengths can be exploited and the weaknesses overcome. But you already know far more about *your* business than anyone else does and must have some ideas about what parts of the business are most critical. What's stopping you from making more money now?

To help to jog your memory, I have listed below a number of the more common causes of poor profitability. Go through each of these in turn and think seriously about whether and to what extent each one applies to your business.

(a) *Customers* – do you need more customers? Could you cope with more if you got them? Do you have as many customers as you can handle but need them to spend more? Are you attracting the wrong kind of customer? Does your trade fluctuate too much? Are you too dependent on one or two large customers?

(b) *Supplies* – are your sales limited by the amount of supplies you can get? Do you have trouble with the quality of supplies, either occasionally or continually? Are deliveries of supplies unreliable?

(c) *Skilled staff* – could you increase your turnover if you could get more skilled staff? Do you have a high turnover of skilled staff? Is there an acute shortage of suitable staff in your area? Do competitors 'poach' staff after you have trained them?

(d) *Equipment* – is any of your equipment worn out or obsolete? Is your volume of business limited by the capacity of your equipment? Are your equipment problems simply due to lack of money or are they more complex? Have you spare equipment capacity which you cannot utilize?

(e) *Space* – could you do more business if you had the space to handle it? Could you profitably use more equipment if you had more room? Is it possible to extend your existing workplace? What prevents you from moving to a larger or more suitable workplace?

(f) *Capital* – how quickly could you increase turnover if you had more capital to invest in equipment or facilities? Could you increase sales if you had more stock? Could you buy on better terms if you had more working capital? Could you increase sales profitably by offering better credit terms?

(g) *Your own time* – could you increase sales if you had more time available? What proportion of your time is spent on 'unproductive' activities? What proportion of your personal workload cannot be done by any member of your staff? Have you seriously tried to reduce your personal workload?

There may of course, be many other items I have not mentioned which are unique to particular businesses. Cast your mind over these other aspects of your business and ask yourself the type of question used above.

At this point, I must seriously warn you not to restrict your reading of subsequent chapters to those aspects of the business which you have picked out as problem areas. The very familiarity you possess with your own business can lead to blind spots. More importantly, a part of the business which you consider is functioning well enough to be ignored may be functioning so well that it can be used as the basis of a profitable sideline. Remember that throughout this book we are looking for strengths as well as weaknesses, opportunities as well as problems.

Learning from experience

Professional trainers concerned with management development in big companies make use of what are called *learning experiences*. In these, the management trainee is assigned to a particular task in which many things happen in a short space of time. Many of these happenings will be new to the trainee. Such a learning experience has two purposes: (a) to allow the trainer to judge the ability of the trainee to cope with new experiences; (b) to broaden the experience of the trainee more rapidly than could be done in a normal job.

If the trainee copes successfully, he adds to his experience, builds up self-confidence and develops more rapidly as a manager. If he handles these experiences badly, his ego is badly dented and he will probably be dropped from the management-development programme. These learning experiences are usually carefully chosen so that even if the trainee is a disaster, little harm befalls the company. This may sound a rough method, but the business world is a rough place and a senior manager must be able to look after himself.

Starting a new business is a non-stop learning experience, a DIY management-development programme. But there are important differences from the big-business set-up.

- You play a dual role, both trainer and trainee. At the same time as you are coping with the experiences, you are trying to observe how well you do it.
- There is no protection for the company. If you don't cope well enough, your business can go bust.
- There is no protection for you. No matter how badly your ego is bruised, you must find the strength from somewhere to bounce back and try again.

As an entrepreneur, you differ from a professional manager in that you are not being developed in the direction which 'big brother' has chosen; you are developing yourself in the direction you choose. But there are still some limitations. Just as the professional manager sacrifices a degree of freedom for the sake of a good career, so must you develop your talents in the direction which best suits your business if you want the latter to prosper.

Let us try to assess just how much you have learned from experience to date by asking the question, 'If you were starting your business all over again, what would you do differently?' Once again, I shall help to jog your memory by listing some aspects of new business where entrepreneurs frequently make mistakes through inexperience. I must stress that it is not a crime to make a mistake. As Samuel Smiles said in his immortal book *Self-Help*: 'We often discover what *will* do, by finding out what will not do; and probably he who never made a mistake never made a discovery'. What *is* a crime is to keep on making the same mistake. So don't be afraid to make a mistake – but be on the look-out to spot when you have made one and correct it promptly, if you can. At least profit from it by being on your guard against repeating it.

(a) *Preparations* – did you overlook any important items? What items did you spend time on which turned out to be unimportant? Were you let down by anyone? How did the actual timing of events compare with what you expected? Were the planning methods you used effective?

(b) *Business experience* – in which aspects of the business has your inexperience led to difficulties? Could you have obtained this experience beforehand (e.g. by previously working for someone else)? Has this lack of experience now been corrected?

(c) *Capital* – did you think you had enough capital before you started? Did you *in fact* have enough? Or did you know you were short but took a chance? Would you take the same chance again? Did you tie up capital unnecessarily, e.g. by buying instead of renting/leasing/HP?

(d) *Facilities* – did you start with adequate facilities – workplace, equipment, fittings? Or did you start on a shoestring, hoping to add more as you needed them? Were you able to add them as needed? Was there anything important you didn't realize you'd need? Did you have any facilities you found you didn't need?

(e) *Stock* – did you have enough stock overall to start with? Were you short of any particular items? In which items did you have too much stock? Did you have problems in getting stock? Did you get good credit terms from the start?

As mentioned above, these are simply some aspects of starting a business, aspects in which mistakes are often made through inexperience. Think carefully over the preparatory period and early days of your business to see what you can add from *your* experience.

It may be that this review leads you to the depressing conclusion that it is time to cut your losses, wind up the business and find something else to do with your time and whatever money is left. This is a sad decision to have to make but sometimes it is the only realistic one – what is sometimes described as the 'least worst' course of action. Hopefully you will conclude that you have a good business, capable of improvement and ready to yield you more money.

If the situation seems less than satisfactory, chapter 19 suggests some ways to change direction towards a more profitable field of operation.

HOMEWORK – CHAPTER I

Since this is a working book, to get full benefit from reading it you must also do some homework. I have found from experience that just thinking about something is not enough; I also need to write it down. Time and again I have gone back over my notes on some topic and found ideas I had completely forgotten about. Indeed, sometimes even after re-reading I still have no recollection of ever writing it down. No doubt your memory is better than mine, but I still suggest that you will benefit by writing down rather than trusting to memory.

It is best to do the homework on each chapter as you finish reading it and before going on to read the next one. In this way, you can record your ideas while they are still fresh. This also makes the results of any calculations available for use when reading the next chapter.

I find that the most convenient method is to use a loose-leaf book, starting a new page for each chapter. This allows you to go back when second thoughts or fresh ideas strike you and write them into the appropriate chapter notes.

To open the volume, here is the homework for chapter 1. This is a rather 'talky-talky' chapter, so try to keep your answers brief.

1-1. Write a brief description of the type of business you are running. Is it making, selling or service?

1-2. Have you ever started a business before? What happened?

1-3. What were your reasons for starting a business now? Why did you choose this business? Do you think you will achieve your objectives?

1-4. What problems, if any, do you have in the following aspects of your business: (a) customers; (b) supplies; (c) skilled staff; (d) equipment; (e) space; (f) capital; (g) your own time; (h) other aspects?

1-5. What have you learned from your experience to date with the following aspects of your business: (a) preparations; (b) business experience; (c) capital; (d) facilities; (e) stock; (f) other aspects?

CHAPTER 2

Sales Figures

In the previous chapter, I asked you to express some views about your business in terms of words. Now we get down to some of the figures. But please don't fall into the trap of thinking that because some aspect of your business can be expressed in numbers, it must be more important than those aspects which can only be expressed in words. It is a very important statement indeed if you can say, 'I'm so glad I started my business – I get a tremendous kick out of it.' Yet there is no way in which that statement can be expressed in figures.

Nor is it true that 'figures don't lie'. Figures can very easily lie if any mistakes are made in collecting, calculating or writing them down. Figures can also mislead if you take the wrong ones for your purpose, e.g. if you forget to correct for VAT in calculating your profit. Nor should you forget the second part of the above statement, '. . . but liars can figure'. Nevertheless, there are so many advantages to be gained from using figures that whenever possible you should express things in numbers.

Which figures?

Figures make it possible to compare the relative importance of different things. For instance, if you have several products or services, you can measure how much sales income comes from each. On the expenditure side, you can see the relative importance of, say, manpower, materials and rent. In addition, it is sometimes possible to find a link between different items, e.g. the increase in sales arising from a specific advertising campaign.

Not only are figures useful, but many people – believe it or not – find them enjoyable. They love to arrange them in different ways just to see what they can find out. This may be quite a useful leisure pursuit for entrepreneurs but it can be carried too far, particularly now that cheap and quite powerful computers are available. So be on guard against crossing the dividing line between 'essential' figures and those that are just 'nice to know'. The calculation may be quick, but you (or your staff) may be spending a lot of time collecting figures just to feed into the computer.

The best safeguard against wasting time with figures is to work out what you want to get from them before deciding when and how to collect them. The first obvious need is for 'total sales' for a given period, the period required obviously depending upon the nature and scale of the business. For instance, it may be a day (retail shop), week (small manufacturer), or month (continuous service).

Important though it is, this single figure doesn't tell us very much about the state of the business. Its usefulness will be much greater if, at the same time, we also get the figures for recent days and weeks (if applicable), for each complete month this year and for each month last year. These figures will show whether overall sales are up or down on last year, and by how much. They will also show how much fluctuation there is in monthly sales and whether it is seasonal or irregular.

Analysis of sales

There are various ways in which total sales can be analyzed to give further insight into the business. If there is more than one *method of selling,* e.g. a retail shop and a mail-order business, the total sales figures described above should be split between the different methods of selling for each period. Not only does this reveal how much each contributes to total sales, but also whether the monthly pattern of sales differs.

If there are *several sales outlets*, e.g. several retail shops, the total sales should be split to produce separate figures for each shop. This is likely to reveal differences due to location, efficiency of shop manager, etc.

Another way of analyzing sales is to split them between *main products/services*. For instance, a car dealer may run his business in three parts: (1) car sales, (2) repair workshop, (3) petrol sales. Although all are on the same site, it is useful to have separate sales figures for each activity. If for no other reason, it makes it much easier to keep a check on the honesty of staff.

Although it is relatively simple to analyze total sales figures if the book-keeping system has been set up to do so, it can sometimes be difficult and time-consuming to produce them in retrospect. With a little ingenuity, however, it is usually possible to produce a reasonable estimate of the breakdown. For example, in the case of the car dealer mentioned above, it is relatively easy, from petrol delivery invoices, to estimate total petrol sales. The car-sales department will have invoices from which to calculate total car sales. The repair workshop will also have invoice records which, although much more voluminous, enable a total to be produced for this activity.

Type of customer

Let me give you a rest from figures for a few minutes. So far in this chapter we have been looking at sales from your side of the counter. Suppose we go over to the other side and look at the viewpoint of the customer. Whatever the nature of your business – making, selling or providing a service – you need to have customers. The type of customer we think of automatically is the public – the person who buys groceries from a shop, phones for the plumber, calls at the garage for petrol. In short, ourselves wearing another hat.

But today there are other types of customer, as many who have started new businesses are aware. It is important to be clear in your mind about the type of customer you are aiming for, since methods which attract one type may not be appropriate for another.

When selling to the *public*, your premises must usually be well lit and decorated in a pleasing fashion. Location may be critical, since many customers put great store on convenience. Consequently, if you want to induce people to come from a distance to your premises, you must have a strong counter-attraction, e.g. very low prices, wide range of stock, easy parking, free delivery, goods not available elsewhere, flexible opening hours, or a combination of these.

When selling to *commercial or industrial companies*, different considerations apply. In the first place, customers may rarely if ever visit the premises, so appearance is less important. Location may still matter, but from the standpoint of distribution cost, not the convenience of the public. Purchasing decisions are likely to be made by technical specialists or professional buyers, rather than laymen. Consequently, although salesmanship is still important, more weight may be put on such factors as product quality, delivery time, price and terms of payment. Moreover, each individual order may be of much greater value and require more effort to secure.

Similar factors may apply when selling to *government departments* or *public corporations*. There is also a greater likelihood of having to tender for a product specified by the customer rather than selling one's own branded product; packaging becomes utilitarian rather than possessing customer appeal. One may also have to submit samples or permit inspection before despatch. Contracts may be for very large quantities phased over a period of time. Cost inflation can erode future profits from such contracts, unless provision is made for price-escalation; fixed-price contracts should be treated with caution.

Local and regional authorities occupy an intermediate position between the two categories. The larger authorities may use tendering and inspection procedures similar to those of government departments, since their purchases are on a similar scale. The small authorities behave more like private-sector companies. Some authorities are very wary about laying themselves open to charges of bribery and corruption, which sometimes makes it difficult to establish personal relations with purchasing officers. On the other hand, most councils are anxious to encourage local enterprises, provided this incurs no extra cost for the ratepayer.

Another point which must be considered is whether your 'customer' is the *ultimate consumer* or a middleman. Do you sell your products to a retailer or wholesaler who, in turn, sells them to the consumer? Are you a subcontractor, providing only part of the final product? Are you paid by some agency to provide a service to a third party?

If your business is of this nature, with no direct contact, you must find some means of getting 'feedback' from the ultimate consumer. What are their real needs? What do they really think of the goods or service you provide? This information may be obtained by market research, by consumer surveys, by reports from salesmen or service engineers, or by a combination of these. It is dangerous to rely solely upon the information you get from the middleman since, by ignorance or design, this may be misleading.

Analysis of customers

Certain quantitative information about customers is useful but may not be available in all businesses. Once again, some ingenuity may be needed to produce what is wanted, or at least a reasonable approximation. Ingenuity may also be required in making the best use of whatever figures are available.

In the first place, if you cater for more than one *type of customer*, as described in the previous section, it is useful to know what volume of sales is made to each type. If your book-keeping system does not produce this easily, it may be possible to pick out the figures from the invoices for a recent period to give a 'snapshot' view.

Next, we want to know the *number of customers* and whether the trend is up or down. There are various ways this can be defined and measured and I suggest you choose the method which requires least extra effort, provided it seems appropriate for your business and allows you to measure the trend. For instance, if you have a relatively small number of large customers, it should be simple to pick out the number of 'active' customers each month from invoice files, sales ledger or computer records. (By 'active', I mean customers who bought something during the period in question.) If you have a retail business with a cash register, the latter may record the number of transactions each day.

A logical follow-on from the above is a calculation of the *average sale per customer*, found by dividing total sales by the number of 'active' customers for the same period. The trends for the above two figures will reveal how rapidly your 'customer base' is growing (or otherwise) and whether your unit sales are keeping up with inflation.

Related to the above is the *repeat business ratio*, in other words how much of your trade arises from old customers coming back and how much from new customers. Of course in some businesses this is almost irrelevant because the time cycle is so long, e.g. furniture removers. Even here, however, there is an indirect assessment by recording which new customers come through personal recommendation. In other cases (e.g. retail trade) it may seem impossible to measure. Nevertheless, if the business is small enough for you to know most of your regular customers by sight, you may be able to estimate how much of a day's trade comes from them.

Bear in mind, however, that too much dependence upon old customers can make you *vulnerable*. This is illustrated by the story of Robert.

> 'I had a very nice little business, rustproofing cars on a franchise basis. It was a sound process and business expanded steadily as the public became more aware of the hazards of body rust. I was particularly pleased when I got my toe in the door with a Ford main dealer, just half a mile down the road. He was a very go-ahead fellow and eventually he accounted for nearly half my trade. Then one Friday he calmly told me that from Monday morning he'd be doing all his own rust-proofing. It nearly broke me at the time and took over two years before I was back to where I had been.'

If one customer accounts for a third or more of your turnover, you are exposed, not only to the risk of closure but, what is much more common, to undue pressure to grant favourable terms to that customer at the expense of your own profit margin.

There is also another, less obvious, form of vulnerability. If a high proportion of your customers are employed by the same factory or office, you may be in serious trouble if it closes down. Cutting out the old customers seems rather like financial suicide and so, in practice, the only remedy for vulnerability is to work hard at broadening the customer base.

Figure control

How much difficulty have you had in digging out the figures discussed above? To some extent, this will depend on the type of business; indeed, some of the figures may not even be appropriate for your business. On the whole, however, the difficulties you find are a reflection of your control system. Are you recording enough figures? More to the point, are you recording the right figures?

Most new businesses start off, quite rightly in my opinion, with too few rather than too many controls. It is much easier to add new controls as you find you need them than to detect and cut out superfluous ones. Nevertheless, I have assumed that the readers of this book have got past the start-up stage. Your business is now established and you may want to make it grow – a situation which needs a different control system.

By controls, I am not referring simply to your financial accounts, although these may form part of your control system. In most businesses, however, there are other figures which are important for judging how well things are going. Some examples of controls are given below.

'I'm Alex and I operate a small taxi business. Next to wages, my biggest item of expenditure is petrol. I pay for this on a monthly account, but my real control comes from a daily calculation of the miles per gallon from each of my taxis over the previous 24 hours. This quickly shows up when any vehicle needs overhaul and, in the longer run, replacement. Incidentally, it also discourages fiddling by the drivers.'

'I'm Vicki. I have a chain of four small boutiques in neighbouring towns. To help me keep right on top of things, each of my manageresses phones in first thing each morning to report the takings and discuss the previous day's business. Contrary to what you might expect, I find that they appreciate the close interest I take and come up with a lot of good ideas.'

'My name is Robin. My wife and I have been in the hotel business for nearly 20 years, and two years ago we took the plunge and bought a hotel of our own. The key to success or failure in this business is room occupancy and we watch this like hawks. Each morning we compare the previous night's figure with the corresponding night for the previous two years to see how much up (or down) we are.'

'I'm Harold. I'm a used-car dealer – one main site and five branches. Each morning I phone my branch managers to check on the state of play. They're very keen to tell me what they've sold the day before, because they're paid on commission. But I'm just as keen to hear the value of the unsold stock. That adds up to my overdraft and with interest rates what they are today, that can really knock my profits.'

These 'cameos' illustrate some points common to most business controls:

(1) each control deals with a factor which has an important effect on the profit of the business;
(2) they are quantitative but not necessarily financial;
(3) they are simple and quick to calculate;
(4) they provide an early-warning system, indicating when action is needed;
(5) they allow comparison between different parts of a business and/or the same business at different times.

As you study your business to decide which of the figures discussed earlier apply to it – and how you are going to get them – you might find it helpful to involve some of your staff. They are 'closer to the ground' than you and may be able to suggest how to produce what you want with least effort. They may even already have records of something pretty close to it

Similarly, when you decide that certain figures are useful on a routine basis, you may again find it helpful to discuss with some of your staff how to produce them regularly. Not only can you use their ingenuity to supplement yours, but the odds are that they will be the ones required to present the figures on a regular basis. They are more likely to be enthusiastic about this if they have had a voice in developing the system.

HOMEWORK – CHAPTER 2

2-1. Tabulate total sales for each month last year and for each complete month this year.

2-2. Study your own business to see if any of the following breakdowns apply: method of selling; multiple-sales outlets; main products/services. If so, try to produce an analysis of the figures given in 2-1. If you have difficulty in finding a way of doing so, discuss with appropriate members of your staff to see if they have any ideas.

2-3. Which type of customer are you supplying? If more than one, try to produce a breakdown of the total sales figures produced in 2-1.

2-4. What evidence have you of customer satisfaction or dissatisfaction with your present product/service? Is this at first hand or via an intermediary?

2-5. Tabulate (if you can) the monthly sales to old and new customers respectively for the past 12 months.

2-6.   Who are your three largest customers? What was the total sales to each during the past 12 months and what proportion of total sales does this represent?

2-7.   What special business controls do you use?

CHAPTER 3

The Market

The fact that you have survived so far and are thinking about expanding shows there must be at least a reasonable market for your product or service. But before committing effort and resources to making your business grow, you want to know how much scope there is for future growth. You might be getting close to the limit already. It is therefore necessary to try to get some figures on just how big the market is in total, what share you have, and the relative strength of your competitors.

This is unlikely to be easy and the answers you get may not be very precise. As long as you are aware of the limits of accuracy, however, approximate figures are better than flying blind. Fortunately there is often more than one way of estimating demand and so you can cross-check your figures.

Estimating the market

For many types of business, the first step in estimating market demand lies in spotting how the market is related to something you can easily find out, such as groceries (total population), maternity wear (number of births), carpets (number of new houses), home insurance (number of households), office stationery (number of businesses). A little ingenuity may be needed to find the link between your product or service and some publicly available statistic, but a careful review of your customers might reveal a common thread.

Then you decide upon your 'effective sales territory',

i.e. the area within which most of your customers will be located. You then find out from local-authority or government sources the figures for population, houses, births or whatever you seek within your territory. If you don't know where to find this information, your local library is usually an excellent starting point.

Finally you estimate the annual expenditure within your sales territory on your particular product or service. In many cases this can be obtained from the Family Expenditure Survey issued by the Department of Employment and published by HMSO. Copies of this are usually available in the larger libraries.

In other cases, such an approach does not help. If your business is a highly specialized one, territory may have little significance, since you and/or the customer may be prepared to travel considerable distances to do business. Or, if you operate a mail-order business, your territory could be the whole country. This makes it more difficult but you may be able to get useful information from the nearest regional Small Firms Centre (Freefone 2444), your Local Enterprise Agency (if you have one), or your trade association. In addition, articles in trade journals sometimes give statistics. Whatever method you adopt, it is worth some effort to get some quantitative information about the total market for your product or service. What share of this market have you got?

Competition

It is of course unlikely that you have no competitors and by now you are probably well aware of who they are. Mark your territory on a map and plot the position of each. How well entrenched are they? What is the reputation of each? Don't forget also that there may be other firms which, although outside your territory, can still be effective competitors. For instance, some of the large shopping centres attract customers from a considerable distance for major shopping expeditions. There may also be goods in your line of business included in the catalogues of the large mail-order companies. If so, you should glance through them occasionally to see what they offer and how their prices compare with yours.

Now we come to the more difficult part – what share of the total market within your territory do you reckon each of them has? If any are public limited companies, you can get hold of their annual report and accounts, which may give details of turnover. Of course, such companies often have more than one location and may have a bigger range of goods and services than you. Nevertheless, you may be able to do some judicious estimating from the figures provided.

You should visit all your competitors' premises periodically and have a good look round outside and, if possible, inside. You may be able to estimate turnover from the area, stock, staff and number of customers. Chatting up the suppliers' representatives and delivery men may provide information on your competitors' purchases. Some of your customers may let slip remarks about your competitors. Regular study of their advertisements may provide a lot of information on their activities. Caution must be used in drawing conclusions from much of this information, since guesses may be reported as fact and some of your informants may deliberately deceive, for various motives. Cross-check whenever you can.

Class of market

So far, I have been talking about the total market as if it were uniform. As you well know, for many products and services this is not the case. There may be a whole range of market quality from the 'bespoke' luxury articles, through various good-quality products to cheap mass-produced things. Associated with this range of product quality is a range of sales service from leisurely individual attention, through brisk but efficient assistance to austere self-service.

Whereabouts in this spectrum does your business lie? Which *class of market* do you aim for? It is important to have this clear in your mind, since so many aspects of business are affected by it: location and decor of premises, number and type of staff, style of advertising, even the design of your stationery and the colour of your wrapping paper.

You must be absolutely consistent in thinking through the implications of the class of market you have selected. If you fail in this, many potential customers who would be pleased by your product or service are put off before they even reach the stage of buying. What is worse, they may tell their friends what a terrible business you run even if they haven't bought. Unjust, perhaps, but the business world is a hard place. Some entrepreneurs have a flair for knowing just the right way to do things. Lucky old them – the rest of us just have to think it through.

Since your reasons for selecting that class of market may influence the development of your business, let us spend a few minutes on this topic. In many cases, the main reason is temperamental, as the following three cases demonstrate.

Tony says, 'I detest snobs and their condescending ways. I also despise the masses and their vulgar tastes. I realize, of course, that I'm in business and have to be polite to every customer – but I can choose the kind of business I want. I run a furniture store selling good-quality, middle-of-the-road merchandise, neither antiques nor treacle and plastic rubbish. I sell the kind of stuff I like myself and it attracts customers who are the kind of people I like.'

Jennifer says, 'I run an interior-decorating business. While my assistant runs the shop, I spend most of my time in my studio, at clients' houses or on the prowl round the dealers. I adore working with beautiful materials and objects, so much so that I'm willing to put up with the foibles of my customers. Some can be real battle-axes, but as long as they'll foot the bill for letting me create something beautiful, why should I care?'

Pete says, 'I run a DIY supermarket which I've built up from a market stall. Now I can buy on a big enough scale to compete with the chains that advertise on TV. My aim is to supply the ordinary man in the street with the means to make his own home look just as good as those in the glossy women's magazines. I reckon if I treat him fair, he'll treat me fair. I may be advertising on TV myself one day.'

If you find that one of the above examples rings a bell with you, then you will probably not feel at ease if you switch to another class of market. You had better stick to your existing type of customer and look for new products or services you can offer them. On the other hand, you may have chosen this class of market for one of a number of dispassionate reasons. In which case, you will have no temperamental objection to changing to another class of market, provided there is a good reason for doing so.

Your survey of competitors needs to be looked at again in the light of the above. If you estimate what share of the total market demand can be allotted to your class of market, well and good, but this is often difficult. You may be lucky if the original figure has been derived from the Family Expenditure Survey. Different tables give figures for different categories of households, according to such things as income, the occupation of the head of the household and the age of the head of the household. See if your class of market approximates to one of these categories.

Market trends

You have now had a good look at the market in your sales territory, both in total and in your own class of market. You know who your competitors are and have a good idea of how you compare with them in terms of turnover. But this is just a snapshot of what the market was at a particular moment in time. In fact, depending upon your sources of information, some of the figures may be representative of the situation one or two years ago rather than today.

The whole purpose of your reading this book is not to study the past but to learn how to make your profits grow in the future. So the snapshot you have built up of the present (or recent past) has now to be transformed into a video of the future. The simplest and most obvious approach is to take the trend of demand for, say, the last five years and see how the figures would look if this continued for the next five years.

During the fifties and sixties, this approach would have been good enough for most businesses. That was when we 'never had it so good'. Things began to go adrift in the seventies and have not yet recovered, but it is still worth a simple experiment. Government and trade organizations produce annual statistics for total national demand for a wide range of activities. See if you can obtain the figures for the last five years for your business – or something closely related to it. If you are lucky, they will show a steady upward trend. More likely, they will show a downward trend, a U-shape, or a random scatter.

However the figures look, even with a steadily rising trend, it is no longer safe to assume that such a trend will continue on the same scale in future. On the other hand, no matter how irregular the pattern, the figures are by no means useless. If you have been running your business for any length of time, you have probably developed a fairly good qualitative 'feel' for the market. You know the things customers like (or dislike) about the products or service you offer, and you have a shrewd idea how these tastes will change in the near future.

To exploit the market successfully, it is necessary to develop this 'feel' on a more *quantitative* basis. To feel that demand is going to rise is not enough. You want to know roughly how fast – is it 5 per cent per annum, 10, 20, 50, 100 – or what? Similarly, if it is going to drop, then at what rate? If it is going to wobble about without a clear movement either up or down, within what range will it do this?

'This is impossible,' you may exclaim. 'No one can predict exactly what is going to happen in the future'. I agree. But most successful businesses have been built by someone who was right more times than he was wrong; someone who had thought through what was most likely to happen and was prepared for it, so that he was ready to take advantage of it before his competitors realized what had happened. Of course luck comes into it too – but luck tends to come to the person who is looking for it and is ready to make the most of it. You are not trying to guess exactly what will happen. You are simply trying to guess more accurately than your competitors.

There are usually various factors affecting future demand, some of which may be positive and some negative. Unless one has a rough idea of the quantitative effect of each, it is not possible to work out whether the overall balance will result in an increase or decrease. At the beginning of this chapter, I pointed out that the first step in estimating demand is often to spot the link between your market and something for which statistics are readily available. Since this is often one of the factors influencing your market demand, a study of this is likely to throw some light on what is likely to happen in your market in the near future.

Population trends

Many products are linked to people and many services are carried out for people. It is not surprising, therefore, that one of the most common factors to influence demand is *population,* either in total or a particular segment, defined by age or sex. Fortunately, forecasts of future population trends are readily available, since population projections are prepared each year by the Government Actuary, in consultation with the three Registrars-General. These are published in summary form each year in the *Annual Abstract of Statistics* and in *Social Trends.*

Any projection is very dependent upon the assumptions on which it is based, and sometimes a range of projections may be explored by trying the effect of different assumptions. In this case it is considered more suitable to produce a single 'official' set of projections to provide consistency between the many users.

Nevertheless, the Government Actuary feels it necessary to issue the warning that the reader should 'constantly bear in mind that any set of projections is based on a particular set of assumptions which are almost certain to be proved incorrect to a greater or lesser degree, even though at the time they were adopted they were judged to be the best that could be made'.

Taking the Government Actuary's warning very much to heart, I give below some of the highlights from *Social Trends (1984).*

The population of the United Kingdom grew steadily from 1901 (38.2 million) to 1971 (55.6 million) but since then the overall totals have remained fairly level with only slow growth projected for the years up to the end of the century. Some details of this are given in Table 3-1: Sex and age structure of the population.

Table 3-1: Sex and age structure of the population (millions)

Age	mid-year		Projections							
	1981		1986		1991		1996		2001	
	M	F	M	F	M	F	M	F	M	F
0–4	1.7	1.6	1.9	1.8	2.1	2.0	2.2	2.0	2.1	1.9
5–15	4.5	4.3	4.1	3.8	4.0	3.7	4.3	4.1	4.6	4.4
16–29	5.9	5.7	6.3	6.1	6.1	5.9	5.5	5.3	5.0	4.9
30–44	5.4	5.3	5.7	5.7	5.9	5.9	6.1	6.1	6.4	6.4
45–59	4.6	4.7	4.6	4.7	4.7	4.8	5.1	5.2	5.3	5.4
60–64	1.3	1.5	1.5	1.6	1.4	1.5	1.3	1.4	1.3	1.4
65–74	2.2	2.9	2.2	2.8	2.2	2.8	2.2	2.7	2.1	2.6
75–84	0.9	1.7	1.1	1.9	1.1	2.0	1.1	1.9	1.2	1.9
85+	0.1	0.5	0.2	0.5	0.2	0.6	0.3	0.7	0.3	0.8
sub-tot	26.6	28.1	27.4	29.0	27.7	29.2	28.0	29.5	28.3	29.7
Total	54.7		56.4		56.9		57.5		58.0	

Source: *Social Trends (1984)* – Table 1.2
(N.B. Figures for 1981 are for GB only, the others are for UK – just one of the pitfalls in using statistics)

The number of pre-school-age children is now on the increase and is likely to continue growing throughout the 1980s. Numbers in the compulsory school age range, particularly those over 11, are expected to continue falling until about 1990. As time passes, these generations of children will come into the market for employment and for housing. For example, over the next few years there will be fewer young people approaching school-leaving age and beginning to look for a job or further education.

The number of people aged 65 or over has grown by over 2 million since 1961 but is not expected to increase much more up to the end of the century. This is due to the low birth rates in the late 1920s and 1930s. However, the balance of age-groups is expected to change. Those aged 65–74 are projected to make up 53 per cent of the 65+ population in 2001, compared with 62 per cent in 1981. Those aged 85+ are projected to make up 12 per cent of the elderly, compared with 7 per cent in 1981. This will lead to greater calls on the health and social services, as it is the oldest people who tend to need these services, rather than the more active 65–74-year-olds.

Table 3-2: Births, deaths and migration (thousands)

	AVERAGE ANNUAL CHANGE				
Projection	Live births	Deaths	Net natural change	Net migration	Overall change
1981–1986	744	670	74	–51	23
1986–1991	831	687	144	–35	109
1991–1996	853	693	160	–35	125
1996–2001	810	689	121	–35	86

Source: *Social Trends (1984)* – Table 1.7

Table 3-2 illustrates how the different factors which determine the size of the UK population – births, deaths, migration – are expected to change. While population loss due to deaths and net migration is projected to remain fairly steady up to the end of the century, births are projected to rise until the mid-1990s, giving slow growth in the population overall, from 56 million in 1981 to about 58 million in 2001.

Table 3-3: Regional and national trends (millions)

Countries/ Regions	mid-year estimates			Projections		
	1961	1971	1981	1986	1991	2001
England						
North	3.1	3.1	3.1	3.1	3.0	3.0
Yorkshire/ Humberside	4.7	4.9	4.9	4.9	4.9	5.0
East Midlands	3.3	3.6	3.9	3.9	4.0	4.1
East Anglia	1.5	1.7	1.9	2.0	2.0	2.2
South East	16.1	17.0	17.0	17.2	17.4	17.9
South West	3.7	4.1	4.4	4.4	4.5	4.8
West Midlands	4.8	5.1	5.2	5.2	5.2	5.3
North West	6.4	6.6	6.5	6.4	6.3	6.3
	43.6	46.2	46.8	46.9	47.5	48.6
Wales	2.6	2.7	2.8	2.8	2.8	2.9
Scotland	5.2	5.2	5.2	5.1	5.1	5.0
N. Ireland	1.4	1.5	1.6	1.5	1.5	1.5

Source: *Social Trends (1984)* – Table 1.9
  (N.B. Some of the totals for England do not agree with the sum of the regions. This is presumably due to rounding off.)

Table 3-3 shows recent changes in the population of the constituent regions and countries of the United Kingdom and the projected changes to 2001. The South West and East Anglia, both predominantly rural areas, are the regions with the greatest growth since 1961. Not shown on the table is the fact that the slow growth of the South East masks the fact that the population of Greater London has dropped from 8.0 million in 1961 to 6.8 million in 1981 and is projected to remain at this level. There has been a general movement away from cities to the country.

Other factors

Although undoubtedly important, population is not the only factor which must be considered in trying to forecast future market demand. In many cases it may not even be the most important. For instance, with a relatively new product or service you must consider the *product-development curve*. When a new product (or service) appears on the market, many people don't know about it, it is often expensive and sales are small. If it is a good product and well marketed, sales increase, together with production capacity. Then more entrepreneurs jump on the bandwagon; competition pushes prices down and sales up.

Eventually, nearly everyone who is likely to want one has one and sales drop. We say the market has reached *saturation* and future sales level out on a replacement basis, i.e. just enough to replace the ones which wear out. The car industry is an example of such a market. Of course, this need not be the end of the story. One can start exporting to other countries at an early stage of the product-development curve.

Alternatively, such a big step may be made in developing the product that everyone wants to throw out the old one and buy a new one, e.g. when colour TV replaced black and white TV. These examples show how critical it is to recognize whereabouts on the product-development curve your market and product lie, and whether your business is up front with the leaders, in the middle of the pack, or trailing along behind.

Sometimes a new product comes in like a whirlwind and out again just as quickly, e.g. hula hoops. Such a product seems to follow a *fashion curve* rather than a product-development curve. There is not time for many entrepreneurs to join in and very fast footwork indeed is needed in both entering and leaving the market. Those who are not nimble enough either never get in or, perhaps worse, are left with a lot of unsaleable stock when the party is over.

Many businesses suffer from a considerable amount of *indirect product competition,* the extent of which is not always realized. One of the most rapidly growing market sectors in the last ten years is what might loosely be termed 'home improvement'. The following are only some of the products and services which are jostling each other for whatever money the householder can be cajoled into spending to make his house more beautiful/comfortable/impressive/spacious/valuable, etc.

Central heating, DIY shops, double glazing, furniture stores, garden centres, handymen, home magazines, interior decorators, jobbing builders, kitchen and bathroom specialists, landscape gardeners, prefabricated house-extensions, self-assembly furniture, swimming-pools, tennis courts.

Nor does the competition end there. There can be a 'knock-on effect', such as the cash for a particular 'home improvement' being obtained by postponing replacement of the family car – or vice versa. The recent home-improvement boom might also be linked to the poor state of the caravan and boat markets. After all, one gets tax relief on loans for the former but not the latter.

Finally, although by no means the least important factor, comes *economic conditions*. Anyone who has survived in business during the last few years doesn't need to be told that. Not that every business is automatically worse off when hard times come – fillet-steak sales may drop but sausage sales go up. But there are very few businesses not affected in some way by economic conditions.

In trying to foresee market trends, therefore, one must make some assumptions about the future state of the economy. You should not be too 'gloom and doom', – otherwise you'd never do anything – but be a bit cautious. All entrepreneurs take risks but the successful ones don't take avoidable risks.

HOMEWORK – CHAPTER 3

3-1.   What is your estimate of the total market at present for your product or service within your effective sales territory? What share of the market have you got?

3-2.   Who are your main competitors within your sales territory? What is your estimate of the turnover of each? Draw up a list of your competitors according to size of turnover, starting with the biggest, and fitting your business in at the appropriate level.

3-3.   Have you any competitors located outside your sales territory? Who are they and have you any idea of how much they sell within your territory?

3-4.   Describe briefly your class of market. What are your reasons for choosing this class of market?

Have you any objection to changing to another class of market if it looks attractive?

3-5. Look again at the list of your competitors produced in item 3-2. Which of them compete wholly or in part in your class of market? Can you estimate how much of their turnover refers to your class of market? Insert this figure in brackets against each one.

3-6. Make a graph of the national demand for each of the last five years for the nearest approximation of your business that you can find. Using these figures and your own experience, draw on the same graph what you think the trend is likely to be over the next five years. If you think it will be irregular, draw two dotted lines to show the upper and lower levels you expect.

3-7. Describe the 'population' your customers belong to in terms of age, sex, geographical area and any other features. Using the sources described in this chapter, list the projection for your 'population' over the next 15 years. Is it growing or declining? Are there any changes of direction during that period?

3-8. How do you think demand will change over the next five years? Do you foresee any possibility of a dramatic new development which might change your forecast?

3-9. Is your business subject to any indirect product competition? What form does this take? Do any of these have any advantages (e.g. exemption from tax, VAT) compared with your business? Are any growing more rapidly than your market?

3-10. Forecasts of economic conditions are produced by the government, the CBI and various other bodies. Applying your own judgement to these, what do you think conditions are likely to be over the next 2–3 years?

CHAPTER 4

The Money Picture

Accountants recognize two forms of money – *revenue* and *capital*. Revenue is money moving in and out of the business, such as sales income, wage payments, purchase of goods. Capital is money tied up in the business in the form of *fixed capital* (premises, equipment, etc.) or *working capital* (stocks of goods, debts, etc.). The distinction between revenue and capital is important since it affects the calculation of your profits and your tax liabilities. In this chapter we shall build up a picture of how your business stands today in terms of both revenue and capital.

Operating budget

The most useful form in which to construct a picture of your revenue is as an operating budget. Since you will also use this in later chapters, it is worth taking a bit of trouble to make it as accurate as possible. If you already have a budget in some form, then the task should be fairly easy. To avoid any confusion, the items of income and expenditure mentioned before should be entered when incurred, not when paid. The cash-flow budget will be discussed later in the chapter.

Rule a large sheet of paper into fourteen vertical columns: one for the list of items, one for each of the next twelve months and one for the annual total. Under the heading 'Income' list your estimated turnover for each month (less any sales commission and discounts) plus any other sources of business income. To keep this simple it is better to deduct VAT from both income and expenditure. If you are not registered for VAT then obviously you should not deduct it from expenditure since you cannot recover it.

Under the heading 'Expenditure', list all the items associated with running the business, such as: salaries, wages and related costs (NI contributions, luncheon vouchers, expenses, overtime, bonus payments, etc.); goods for sale, raw materials, components; operating supplies; rent, rates and insurance; heating, lighting, telephone, postage, stationery, sundries, advertising, promotion, repairs, spare parts, transport, hire of equipment, bank charges, loan interest, HP payments; other charges.

Deducting expenditure from income gives your *gross profit* for each month and for the year. Pause for a moment to see if there is much fluctuation from month to month. If so, is this inevitable from the nature of your business or might something be done about it?

From the gross profit for the year, you have to deduct *depreciation* or, as the tax inspector calls it, capital allowance. This gives you the *net profit*.

Depreciation is calculated by reducing the value of a capital item (e.g. a machine) by an amount which, each year, represents the ageing and deterioration of the item. Thus, if you believe that a machine will need to be replaced in five years from the time of purchase, then the value of this asset can be reduced, *on your books*, by 20% of the original cost, per annum. This is the so-called 'straight line' depreciation system. You can, if you wish, depreciate in a different fashion, for example by reducing the book value by, say, 40% in the first year, 30% in the next, 20% in the third, and so on.

The purpose of this exercise is to spread the cost of the capital item over a number of trading years so that its effect on profit is not all loaded on the year of purchase. However, this is a somewhat notional process recommended by accountants to reflect true trading results each year. From a *cash-flow* point of view the money is actually spent in the year that the purchase is made, and depreciating an asset is a 'book exercise' only.

It should also be noted that the tax inspector, when deciding capital allowances for the purpose of tax calculation, has his own ideas about how long an item should last and how much allowance can be permitted each year. Your own view as to what is the most sensible and representative rate of depreciation may differ from that of the tax inspector. To prevent confusion it may be better to accept and use the tax inspector's figures.

Cash-flow forecast

By now, your business experience has probably taught you that *profit* is not the only touchstone of success. Equally important – and sometime more so – is *cash flow*. You may have had to wait until a customer's cheque was obtained, perhaps by a personal visit, and 'expressed' through the bank before you could cash a cheque for wages or buy the groceries. Other unfortunates have learned that a business can be trading profitably and yet still go bust because they didn't watch the cash flow. So we shall discuss cash flow too in this chapter.

The purpose of a cash-flow forecast is to plot the month-to-month fluctuations in your income and expenditure. This indicates the tight spots so that you can take avoiding action in advance rather than cope with crises after they have happened. The resulting fluctuations in cash balance, after you have done what you can, give an indication of how much working capital you need.

Take another large sheet of paper, but this time rule it

into thirteen vertical columns: one for the list of items and one for each of the next twelve months. Put the same items in the first column and transpose the figures from the Operating Budget to the Cash-Flow Forecast; only this time put the money figures down for the month when the money is due to be received or paid. Although the turnover is the same for each month, your experience will suggest how much of the money you are likely to receive during the month of sale – some may be received in advance and some a month or more later.

Similarly, with the items of expenditure you will know when the items probably *must* be paid in practice. If some items are paid weekly (e.g. wages), watch for the five-week months and adjust the payments accordingly. Deducting expenditure from income gives the cash-flow balance for each month and whether this is positive or negative.

Study any months which are negative to see if you can make the balance positive by, for example, cutting out or deferring expenditure or spreading it over a longer period. You may also be able to speed up some payments due to you, but the scope for this is usually pretty limited. After you have done all you can in this way, calculate the revised balances for each month.

These figures refer only to the business and must be corrected for what you draw out of the business for living expenses or, alternatively, what you plough into the business from external sources. If you take out a sum each month as *drawings*, you must enter this now on the cash-flow forecast. If it is a fixed sum there is no problem, but if it fluctuates you must estimate it as best you can. If you supplement the business with cash, either continuously or intermittently, this too must be estimated and entered on the sheet.

Finally, you should enter, for the appropriate month,

any special items of income or expenditure which you can foresee, e.g. grants or subsidies, tax bills, vehicle replacement, etc. Add up the new total for each month and, as you do so, check that all the positives and negatives are correct, both for individual items and in adding up the total.

Some of these monthly totals may be negative, but this is of little importance as long as the balance at the beginning of the month is big enough to absorb it. Put down your estimate of the opening balance at the beginning of month 1 and add (or subtract as appropriate) the net total of month 1 to produce a closing balance for that month. For month 2, add (or subtract) the total for that month to the closing balance for month 1 to produce the closing balance for month 2. Continue this for the rest of the twelve months.

Financial prospects

Examination of the monthly closing balances will tell you a lot about your business and its prospects over the next twelve months:

- If they fluctuate, sometimes positive, sometimes negative, but with a fairly level trend, then your business is static but you need more working capital. The biggest deficit which occurs will give you a rough idea of the amount needed.
- If the balances are positive except for one or perhaps two negative months, then your working capital is adequate most of the time but there are one or two tight spots. Make another attempt to smooth them by postponing or spreading out expenditure. If this fails to do the trick, you may need to arrange a short-term loan or overdraft to tide you over the next sticky

period. You'll probably find that showing these calculations to your bank manager will impress him and help you to get the loan.

- If your balances fluctuate, with a level trend, but always comfortably positive, then your business is static but you probably have too much working capital. You can afford to withdraw some working capital and invest it where it will earn interest. Alternatively, you can either invest it in fixed assets, which will reduce your costs, or leave it as working capital and step up the scale of your business.

- If your balances show a steadily increasing positive trend, even if they fluctuate, then you are in that most desirable situation – you have a positive cash flow. In effect, the business is generating cash which can be used for its own expansion. Whether you choose to do so or leave the business ticking over while you 'milk' it of the surplus cash is a topic we shall discuss in a later chapter.

- If your balances show a declining trend with progressively more negative months, then your business is heading for trouble. In effect, you will have to keep pumping money into it just to keep it alive. Such a situation calls for urgent and realistic action. Unless you can turn the business round pretty rapidly, the best course is probably to close it down. The sooner you do so, the less you will lose.

If you are inexperienced in making cash-flow forecasts, then it is only common sense to be cautious in your interpretation. You will, however, be surprised how useful the forecasts become as you gain experience in making and interpreting them. Nevertheless, you must remember at all times that they *are* estimates, estimates which are subject to error, to your personal bias and to the unexpected.

Obviously these qualifications apply with greatest force when the forecasts point to the need for a major decision. In such cases, check the forecasts in every way you can and, if they are subject to a range of error, make sure that the conclusions are the same at both ends of the error range. Once the calculations are confirmed, do not flinch from the decision and its consequences.

Cash flow is not, of course, an alternative to *profit*; it is simply another factor which you have to watch when running a business. For survival, you must both make a profit *and* control cash flow. When there is a cash-flow crisis, entrepreneurs may have to cut prices sharply to get some money in, just to avoid going bust at that moment. But if you sell goods at below what it costs to replace them – and you do it too often – you will find that you have merely postponed going bust, not prevented it. Is it not better to control cash flow so that the crisis doesn't arise?

Price, cost and value

The above three words are often used interchangeably in conversation. Their meanings are not identical, however, and to ensure clear thinking on money matters, it is essential to appreciate their differences. *Price* is the amount of money which is paid when something is bought or sold or when a service is provided. An article may have more than one price (e.g. a cash price and a credit price) and, as we all know, the same article may have different prices in different shops. Nevertheless, the price involved in a specific transaction is usually known precisely and is the same for both buyer and seller. *Cost* is the amount of money which must be paid to obtain something. Cost may be the same as price but often is not. For instance, if you buy a piece of equipment, you may pay a certain price (£P). But before you can use it, you have to spend more, e.g. to have it delivered (£D) and fitted (£F). Although its price is £P, its cost is £(P+D+F). This shows how costs can be additive, i.e. the fitted cost is the sum of the price plus delivery cost plus fitting cost.

Value is what something is worth to someone, and an article can be valued in three different ways. *Replacement value* is what it will cost to replace. If it is readily available at the same price as you paid and does not involve extra costs for delivery and fitting, its replacement value is the same as you paid for it. But replacement value, particularly in inflationary times, is often greater than the original price. On the other hand, if the price of something is dropping rapidly (e.g. mini-computers) its replacement value may be lower than the original price.

Sales value is what someone is willing to pay for something. This may be different from replacement value, as in the case of a piece of fitted equipment. For a standard article in regular demand (e.g. a second-hand vehicle), the selling price may be easy to assess. For non-standard articles with an irregular demand, e.g. industrial equipment, the selling price can be hard to predict, as auction realizations often show. Even if the selling price can be estimated, some deduction must usually be made for selling expenses (e.g. advertising, sales commission, transport) to arrive at the sales value.

Utility value is what something is worth under a particular set of circumstances. A car fuse costs only a few pence when you buy a spare at a garage. But when your car breaks down on the motorway on a winter night, its utility value may be very different. Then you will have to pay several pounds to get a message through to a garage and persuade someone to drive out and deliver a fuse.

At this stage you may be wondering where *book value*

comes in, i.e. the value of an item in your account. Book value is the result of applying accounting conventions to prices paid in the past. It is not related to market prices today and if it happens to be the same as one of the above values it is an accident. Book value allows you to calculate the tax consequences of a decision about money, but it does not tell you what the decision should be.

Financial resources

The traditional method of assessing the financial resources of a business is to study the *balance sheet* or, better still, the balance sheets for the last few years, so that the trends can be observed. I am sure you have studied these very thoroughly with your accountant and there is little I can tell you about them. Their purpose, apart from statutory requirements, is to impress outside share-holders, banks and other creditors. They are of little use for actually running a business.

One reason balance sheets are of little use is that they are produced once a year, portraying a snapshot of the resources on a particular day, usually several months previously. The other reason is that, because of the accounting conventions followed in preparing the balance sheet, it does not necessarily give a realistic picture of the real financial resources of the business.

For instance, one of the features that the balance-sheet analyst looks for is 'Current Assets' being greater than 'Current Liabilities', and preferably about double. But conventions dictate that 'Stocks' and 'Debtors' appear under 'Current Assets' and 'Creditors' appears under 'Current Liabilities'. These conventions are based on perfectly sound accounting reasons, but they are completely in conflict with common sense. Anyone with any business experience knows that one of the easiest ways to go bankrupt is to let 'Stocks' and/or 'Debtors' get out of hand, and that it is an unending struggle to prevent this happening.

Similarly, one of the easiest ways to keep a healthy cash balance is not to pay 'Creditors' until the latest possible date.

If the balance sheet is not an effective means of assessing and keeping control of financial resources, how should this be done? I suggest that the answer is to adopt a different approach. Instead of the conventional fixed and working capital one should think in terms of tied and liquid capital. *Tied capital* consists of things which are not in the form of cash or 'near cash'. These include property, equipment, stocks and work in progress. *Liquid capital*, on the other hand, is cash and securities or short-term investments which can be quickly turned into cash.

The various items in the balance sheet are usually valued at *book value*. What basis should be used for tied capital? As described in the section above, there are three different ways in which an article can be valued, depending upon circumstances and the reason for the valuation. For instance, if the business is being valued as a going concern, the tied capital should be estimated on a *replacement-value* basis. On the other hand, if the business is folding up – or you are studying what would happen if it did – then the tied capital should be valued on a *sales-value* basis. This would be under 'distress sale' conditions and the proceeds would probably be considerably below the normal sales value.

The value of liquid capital would, by definition, be the same in either of the above cases. It would be the total cash and bank balances available plus the cash obtained from realization of securities and short-term investments, less any selling expenses, commission, etc. Adding this to the total tied capital would give the financial resources available to the business under the particular conditions studied.

The calculation of the total financial resources is likely to be infrequent and done only when required. Different elements are, however, likely to be calculated with a different frequency. For example, property is unlikely to change in value very rapidly and is expensive to value professionally. Consequently, this is likely to be reviewed only every three or more years. Many items will be reviewed annually, as part of the Annual Accounts. At the other extreme, the cash balance is likely to be checked at least weekly and, in many cases, daily.

Potential resources

So far we have discussed only the financial resources available within the business itself. There may well be other resources which could be made available if necessary. The first obvious source is yourself, if you still have anything left after starting the business. Most people are surprised to discover how much they are worth, so let's try it.

Take a sheet of paper and list what you are worth. Put down all your assets now and we'll sort out later those which are untouchable. To stimulate your thinking, write down the following headings and any others which occur to you. Put against each one its estimated *sales value*, less any selling expenses and HP or credit payments outstanding.

Cash in hand, bank current and deposit accounts, building-society accounts, national and trustee savings bank accounts, savings certificates, premium bonds, unit trusts, stocks and shares, life-insurance policies, pension-fund contributions, house (less outstanding mortgage), car, furniture and furnishings, domestic equipment, clothes, sports and hobby equipment, jewellery, collections of stamps, coins, etc.

If you are married, some of these may be owned jointly with your spouse. Discuss the matter and, if your spouse agrees, draw up three lists – 'his', 'hers' and 'joint'. If your spouse does not want to put his or her resources behind you (or any more of them) then you should make two lists, one for your own resources and one for your share of joint resources.

You may well have gone through an exercise of this nature when you first started your business. If so, you may feel it is unnecessary to repeat it. If it was some time ago, however, this may be a good opportunity to update your figures. For the rest of you, the next step is to decide how much of your personal resources you are willing to devote to the business should it be necessary. The balance you presumably wish to keep apart for other purposes (e.g. children's education, somewhere to live) in the event of a business collapse. The first part should be kept in some fairly accessible form; the balance should be placed where it cannot be touched by the business.

Apart from any additional personal resources which you and/or your spouse can make available, there may be other members of the family who have offered to assist or who, you think, might be persuaded to contribute. Put down their names and the amount you think they might contribute.

Finally, you may think that your bank or some other financial institution might be willing to put up some money to extend your business. Put down their names too and the amount you think they might advance – also the terms you anticipate.

HOMEWORK – CHAPTER 4

4-1. Construct an operating budget for the next 12 months, using the method described in this chapter.

4-2. Construct a cash-flow forecast for the next 12 months, using the method described in this chapter.

4-3. Study the pattern of the monthly closing balances of your cash-flow forecasts. Write down your conclusions about your financial prospects over the next 12 months.

4-4. Have the above studies resulted in any ideas for changes in your business? Write them down.

4-5. Estimate the value of your tied capital. What basis of valuation did you use and why?

4-6. Estimate the value of your liquid capital.

4-7. Add items 4-5 and 4-6 to give your total financial resources. How does this figure compare with that in your last balance sheet?

4-8. Write down the various items of potential resources which apply in your case and your best estimate of the amount: personal resources (excluding those to be kept apart from the business); spouse's resources (amount he/she is willing to make available); other members of the family and friends; financial institutions.

CHAPTER 5

Resources Other than Money

Money by itself is sterile and uncreative. Lock up some money in a safe and what happens? Nothing. In fact, in these inflationary times it simply loses more value the longer you leave it. It is only when money is put to work that it begins to create and multiply. The least active (but not necessarily least profitable) thing you can do with money is to invest it in someone else's activity. However, this book is not written for stock-exchange investors, it is written for entrepreneurs who want to do something themselves with their money – and perhaps other people's money as well.

To run a business, therefore, it is necessary to have resources other than money, resources which can take many forms: ideas, contacts, customers, suppliers, workplace, equipment, staff and – by no means least – your own time and enthusiasm. In many ways these resources are more important than money. They are certainly more creative, since the entrepreneur with the right package of resources is unlikely to have much difficulty in getting money. The man with money but no idea what to do with it will be lucky if he holds on to it.

Ideas

Some people seem to bubble over with ideas, to be able to keep producing them effortlessly. Some of their ideas may be a bit crazy but they produce so many that a fair number turn out to be pretty good. Often someone else takes them up and sometimes makes a lot of money out of them. Have you ever wondered why the idea creators themselves rarely profit from them?

It is chiefly a matter of temperament. The personal qualities needed to produce ideas are very different from those needed to assess ideas and put them into practice. The ideas man gets his fun from generating ideas. He feels exhilarated by the flow of inspiration. He becomes inhibited if he has to pause to judge them good or bad because it stops the flow. He lacks the patience to beaver away at developing one idea – he would much rather think up more new ones.

To apply ideas successfully, one needs good judgement to select which ideas are worth developing and which should be discarded. There is often a lot of dull slogging in the early days, which requires patience and persistence, but ingenuity is also needed to overcome the many problems which arise during development. Technical skills of a practical nature must often be supplied by the developer or his staff. Finally, it takes a lot of time and money to develop an idea to a profitable outcome.

A rough rule of thumb in research establishments is that one idea in ten is worth developing and, of these, only one in ten results in a profitable product. For the entrepreneur, therefore, it is more important to have the skills of the developer rather than the idea producer. Ideas can be supplied by other people but only you can decide whether or not to back them. Some people have the flair to fill both roles, by switching their mood, but even if you are not outstanding at either activity, there are useful techniques which can be employed.

One of the most common and successful techniques for generating ideas is *brainstorming*. Suppose you are looking for ideas on the best way to launch a new product. Take a sheet of paper and draw a line down the middle. Head the left half 'Aspects' and the right half 'Ideas'. On the left-hand side write down all the aspects of the product and its launch, for instance packaging, formulation, advertising, pricing, guest star, demonstration, and so on.

Now sit back and look at what you have written down. Think hard about the first item on your list and in the right-hand column put down all the ideas you can think of relating to the product launch. For example, taking the first item, 'packaging', this might suggest: family economy size, bio-degradable container, different from competitors, copy most expensive, resemble existing products, recycled material, package designer.

During the brainstorming step, you should not attempt to criticize or censor your ideas. Write down everything that comes into your head, no matter how wild it may seem. There is no need to write a long description – just jot down a word or two to remind you of each idea. The whole point is to keep the flow of inspiration going as long as possible. Keep the pot boiling.

You can, if you wish, turn this into a game to play with family, friends or staff. Often a group of people stimulate each other, an idea from one person triggering off an idea from someone else. When the flow dries up, repeat the process with the next item in the left-hand column until you run out of steam once again. Continue in this way until you have covered everything in the left-hand column. You should now have a list of ideas which can be reconsidered at a later stage.

Reputation and Contacts

During the time you have been in business, you will have acquired a certain reputation which, good or bad, is one of your resources. There are three strands to this reputation:

(a) *Business* – What are you like as a firm to deal with? What is the quality of your goods or services? Are you reliable? Do you have a good range of stock? Do you pay your bills on time?

(b) *Professional* – Do you know your trade thoroughly? Are you well qualified (if relevant)? Are you a full member of the appropriate trade or professional organizations? Are your staff well trained and properly qualified?

(c) *Personal* – Are you a pleasant person to deal with – courteous and good-tempered? Are you fair and scrupulously honest? Are you a 'soft touch'? Do you engage in sharp practice? Are you well organized? Are your employees courteous and helpful?

Although these strands are often interwoven, there may sometimes be quite large gaps between them. For instance, your firm may be quite well run because of the efforts of your predecessor or your existing staff, while you yourself don't know the business. Or you can be very knowledgeable about your profession and yet quite unbusinesslike. It is therefore necessary to assess each strand separately and then overall. Remember the old saying that the strength of a chain is that of the weakest link.

In the course of your business, you will have contact with many people in addition to customers: suppliers, delivery men, bank managers and staff, solicitors, accountants, competitors, staff of trade and professional organizations, journalists, police, dustmen, council officials . . . the list is considerable.

It pays to make a good impression on as many of these contacts as possible. You never know when you are going to want a favour from someone and whether this is granted often depends on how you treated that someone previously – before you wanted a favour. You don't have to crawl or be a back-slapper; it is usually enough to be polite to everyone, regardless of position. Of course, if you can manage a smile as well, this goes a long way. It also helps if you can listen as well as talk.

Customers

If you didn't know it before you started your business, you will surely have learned by now that there is one resource which is vital to all business success – customers. In your other life, as a customer, you may think that you choose where and what to buy. But just ask yourself *why* you choose to use a particular business for your goods or service. Is it because you have had satisfactory dealings there before? Is it because friends have recommended it? Is it because you have seen it advertised? Is it because it is located conveniently, or the quality is better, or the prices are lower, or what? Some of these topics have been discussed from various angles in previous chapters. Here let us bring them together to try to get an overall picture of what it is that attracts customers to *your* business. How have you created the resource that your present customers represent?

Building up a circle of customers by word-of-mouth recommendation is a slow process, although it is the only effective (or permissible) method in some professions. In most other trades and professions, it is customary to accelerate this process by *sales promotion*. The methods most suitable for your business will largely be dictated by the type of customer you want and the class of market you aim to serve. These have already been discussed in chapters 2 and 3 respectively.

The methods you actually use will, however, be influenced by cash availability, and you may feel that, although they are not ideal, they are the best you can afford. The only way to be sure is to do a survey from time to time, comparing your expenditure on sales promotion with the number and type of customers it attracts. Think also about the alternatives.

Many entrepreneurs tend to rely overmuch on 'sales promotion' (rather than 'salesmanship'), particularly when they have had no previous sales experience. They persuade themselves that, with the first-class product and excellent service they offer, there is no need for all that high-pressure stuff. 'Good wine needs no bush', they quote. In many cases they are being dishonest and won't admit to themselves that they lack the courage to approach a stranger and ask him to buy. They foster an image of the salesman being 'brash' or 'smooth'. They don't want to be like that, they think, but secretly they are afraid.

Sales promotion is a method of preparing the ground, but unless it is followed up by active salesmanship the results will be small. Advertising may cause someone to enter your shop but you still have to sell once he gets there, otherwise he may go out empty-handed and never return. A mailing shot may make potential customers aware of your business, but unless you follow up with a personal approach they will have forgotten it by the time they need your services. So when you make your survey of sales promotion, look also at how effective you have been in converting initial contacts into real customers.

Workplace and equipment

Many businesses can be started in a dining-room or garage, but by the time they are providing a decent living they have usually grown to the stage of needing a separate workplace – be it shop, office or workshop – with some equipment. The book cost of this resource will appear in your balance sheet, but its real value to you can be much more than this – or less.

Obviously *location* is critical for the success of many businesses, e.g. newsagent/tobacconist at a bus station, transport company at a motorway junction. Nevertheless, it is possible to pay too much even for a prime site, and a high level of fixed costs is hazardous for your company. Where location does not have much effect on sales volume, a prime site is an extravagance to be avoided, although location can affect other factors besides customers, e.g. access for supplies, staff transport, surrounding environment.

No workplace is perfect – at least not one you can afford – and in terms of *facilities* some degree of 'trading off' always seems to be necessary. If the heating and lighting are adequate, the car park is too small; if the turning circle is ample for suppliers' lorries, the roof leaks. By the time one has survived a full annual cycle in a workplace one knows whether, on balance, it is a good one or a bad one.

There is a limit to the extent to which the *layout* of any existing building or yard can be altered. Once you have moved in and installed your equipment and fittings, you have even less freedom to change. If the building was the right shape and you were clever in planning where to put equipment and fittings, you have an advantageous layout. But in an awkwardly shaped building with badly placed equipment, you may be working under difficulties all the time. And yet two different workplaces may have the same nominal floorspace and rent.

If you bought most of your *equipment* secondhand and you have kept it in good condition, it is probably worth much more to you than its book value. But the buying price is only one consideration; perhaps even more important is whether it is the right equipment for your business. It is easy to be pressured into buying what the salesman wants to sell you rather than what you really need, especially if you are not sure of the latter. If you bought new equipment which is unsuitable, you will lose a lot of money when you sell it. Nevertheless, if you can replace it with the right goods secondhand, you may not be too much out of pocket. Needless to say, if you lack the personal expertise, you should get a reliable mechanic to check any secondhand equipment *before* you buy it.

Supplies and stocks

Broadly speaking there are three main types of supplies: consumable materials (e.g. stationery, lubricants, cleaning materials); raw materials and components; goods for resale. The proportions of these three types obviously vary widely from one type of business to another, but there are few businesses where expenditure on supplies is unimportant. Indeed, in many types of business, shrewd buying makes all the difference between profit and loss.

When you started your business, you had to find out the right suppliers for *your* business, ones who were reliable and who would supply what you wanted, when you wanted it, at reasonable prices. This is a trial-and-error activity and some error is almost inevitable. In short, you paid a price for learning which suppliers to use, and this knowledge is now one of your resources.

Consumable materials are a small proportion of expenditure in most businesses. This does not mean that you should ignore the cost but you should keep a sense of proportion. Unless the quantities are large, and significantly better terms can be obtained elsewhere, it is better to stick to local suppliers for these goods. It is an inexpensive way of building up goodwill in the local community and may create business for you. In business terms, this is called *reciprocity*; in everyday terms it is called 'you scratch my back and I'll scratch yours'.

Raw materials and components warrant a lot of attention in most manufacturing businesses. Not only are they likely to be a significant item of expenditure, but faults may cause difficulties during your manufacturing process or give rise to complaints from your customers. Have you found satisfactory suppliers for all important items? Do you still have any quality or delivery problems?

Goods for sale represent the biggest single item of expenditure in many businesses and thus deserve a lot of attention. Your buying policy must be firmly based on your business strategy. Are you selling high-quality goods at a reasonable price, or are you selling run-of-the-mill articles as cheaply as possible? Do you aim to keep a wide range in stock at all times, or concentrate on a limited range of fast-selling items? Are you competing mainly on price, or do you provide certain services, e.g. customer advice, free delivery, free installation?

Your buying policy should also reflect your customers' buying habits. If you want to build up a group of regular customers who look to you as the 'natural' place to buy certain goods, then you must build up a group of regular suppliers. If you aim to provide quickly those items not in stock, then you must find suppliers who provide a similar service. If you rely on attracting casual customers by large discounts, you must find sources of low-price goods.

Most entrepreneurs start with low stocks, partly of necessity because cash is scarce, and partly to minimize the risk of buying the wrong materials. As the business grows, stocks usually increase, partly as the cash becomes available and partly in response to customer demand. Sometimes stocks grow for another reason, however, as the volume of slow-moving and unsaleable goods increases. This is a fatal mistake. Not only do such goods represent money which you could well do with, but they tie up space, facilities and staff time. You must be absolutely ruthless in clearing out such material. At least once a year you must dispose *completely* of all dead stock for the best price you can get, however low that may be. The Inland Revenue bears part of the loss, since it is offset against profits, and you have the immediate use of the cash and storage space. You probably also do a lot of good for your image among both customers and staff.

Your own time

One of the major resources in your business is your own time. This is often the barrier to further expansion of the firm, and I wonder if there are any readers who have never said, 'Oh, for a few more hours in the day.' You may think you know how you spend your time at present. This is probably untrue but don't take my word for it. Try this little experiment. Write down on a piece of paper the activities on which you spend most of your time, and add a further item for 'other activities'. Put against each the percentage of your time that you spend on that activity and put the paper in a drawer.

Now keep a detailed record for a week using a technique called activity sampling. Take a sheet of paper for each day, mark the time at quarter-hour intervals down the left-hand side, and rule a column for each of your selected activities, plus an extra one for 'other activities'. Every quarter of an hour (or thereabouts) put a tick under the heading for what you are doing at that moment. At the end of each day, count the number of ticks under each heading; then total them for the week and calculate the percentage of the total for each activity.

If the result of this experiment tallies with your estimate, then you are one of those rare individuals who really does know how he spends his time. You are more likely to be surprised and perhaps disappointed. Indeed, in my own case, I had to do a second run with a different set of headings to break down the large percentage under 'other activities'. This experiment will have taught you a little about your present time usage and perhaps convinced you that you could improve upon it.

Staff

One obvious way of saving some of your own time is to pay someone else to do some of your work. Indeed, very many entrepreneurs do this. They also hire staff to do jobs they can't do themselves. Slowly the entrepreneur builds up a team of supporters. But many things about a new business cannot be done the ideal way and staff is rarely built up in a systematic, carefully planned manner.

As a rule, you can't afford to take on people until you really need them and by that time you need them fast. So if you can't get someone who fits the bill exactly, you take the next best. If they turn out wrong, you get rid of them and hire someone else. Gradually, by trial and error, you build up a team that suits you. They may not be perfect but they are adaptable and work well together.

To be in at the start of a new business is an exciting experience which develops a close camaraderie among the people involved, regardless of the position. Now along comes the management consultant and threatens to spoil it all. He tells the owner to remove his rose-tinted spectacles, just for a moment, and look at his staff as employees, rather than comrades. Because the owner has a unique responsibility: the future of the business and of his staff rests upon his decisions – and his alone.

So take some time to do a *staff inventory*. First of all look at the total staff. Do you really need the number you have? How much extra business could you handle without taking on more staff? What are the staff bottle-necks where trouble first shows up when you are heavily loaded? Can you rearrange duties to increase capacity at this point? Could you train more of your staff to help out at the bottle-neck?

Now do an inventory on each individual, trying to forget how long he or she has been with you and the escapades you have shared. If you had experience in writing staff reports before you started your own business, you will know the kind of thing that is wanted. If not, you will find it helpful to get a management book from the library which deals with staff-report writing. Writing comments in response to a stereotyped form will help you to think more dispassionately.

What you are interested in firstly is their knowledge and skills. What talents do they have which are useful to the business? Have they any which are not at present used but might be? Are they lacking any which would make them more useful? Could this lack be remedied by training, either within the business or with some outside body? Secondly – and no less important – you are interested in them as people. Here you will find a conventional staff report doubly useful, both as a check-list and to help you compare people on a standard basis. You must judge what their strong and weak points are and how well they are suited to their role in the business, which employees are capable of taking on more responsibility as the business grows, and which have already reached their limit.

Now turn back again to the business as a whole. Does the team really run as smoothly as you sometimes think or is there some friction beneath the surface here and there? Can this be put right by rearranging duties? Do you need to 'talk to' one or two people, or would it be wiser to ease out the potential trouble-makers before the business gets any bigger? In what aspects of the business is your staff strongest? Where are your weaker points? Can these be overcome by training existing staff or should you recruit new staff?

HOMEWORK – CHAPTER 5

5-1. Try a brainstorming exercise to produce ideas on 'How to make more money from my business'. You may find it more fruitful if you do two exercises: (a) alone, (b) jointly with your staff.

5-2. Write down what you think your reputation is in terms of: (a) business; (b) professional; (c) personal; (d) overall. How accurate do you think your own assessment is?

5-3. Describe any sales-promotion campaign you have conducted for your business. How successful was it? How did you follow up? How appropriate was it for your type of customer and class of market? What did you learn from it?

5-4. Divide a sheet of paper into two columns headed 'Advantages' and 'Disadvantages'. Write down your comments on your existing workplace under the sub-headings: (a) location; (b) facilities; (c) layout; (d) equipment; (e) other factors. If your business grows, should you keep it or find a new one?

5-5. How much do you spend per annum on *consumable materials*? What percentage is this of total expenditure? Where do you buy most of them?

5-6. How much do you spend per annum on *raw materials and components*? What percentage is this of total expenditure? What problems do you experience with suppliers?

5-7.   How much do you spend per annum on *goods for sale*? What percentage is this of total expenditure? What problems do you experience with suppliers?

5-8.   Conduct the time-record experiment described in the chapter. Are you satisfied with the result? If not, what would you like to change in your time-pattern?

5-9.   Write up staff inventories as described in the chapter for both total staff and individuals. As a result of this, what action do you think you should take?

PART 2
How to Increase Income

CHAPTER 6

Increasing your Sales

The simplest way to make more money from your business is to increase your sales turnover – simple, but perhaps not so easy. The purpose of this chapter is to discuss ways of increasing turnover. The obvious method is just to increase prices, although this might have the reverse effect, viz. a drop in turnover. Fear of this causes many small businesses, particularly in the service sector, to lose out because they are afraid to charge enough.

After a careful study of competitors' prices in your sales territory, you may decide you will lose sales if you increase *your* prices. If so, let it be a deliberate decision, not just a lack of courage combined with a failure to face reality. Remember that your low-priced competitors are not necessarily more efficient than you – they may just be less intelligent. Consequently, if you decide you can't increase prices above a level at which you are losing money, then you had better think about packing it in. You are not obliged to continue running at a loss.

This may of course be just what one of your competitors is trying to make you do. If he has strong financial reserves, he may decide to run at a loss for a time to force some of his weaker competitors out of business. Then he would hope to raise his prices and recover his losses. This 'crafty' price-cutting can happen but is much less common than 'stupid' price-cutting.

If you have studied your competitors as described above (Homework 3-2, 3-5), you should not find it difficult to decide which situation applies in your case. You must then decide whether or not you can afford to stay in and fight. Try to be realistic and unemotional in this decision. If you are going to cut your losses, the quicker you do it the better, so that you can salvage as much as possible for a fresh start in some other line.

On the other hand, if you still make a reasonable profit at present prices, then you can turn your attention to the other alternative – increasing sales volume. Some of the ideas discussed in the rest of this chapter may seem more appropriate to a 'selling' business than to 'making' or 'service' but, whatever your business, think hard about all the ideas in this chapter to see which could be applied to your business. This applies also even if you do increase prices, because increasing sales volume is the only long-term road to growth.

Increasing existing sales

The first step towards increasing sales volume is to take a systematic look at how you can increase sales of existing products or services through existing outlets using the existing organization. Changes in this area are unlikely to be expensive and can probably be introduced quickly.

What can you do to make people buy more? Can you change the quality (and price?) moving either up or down market? Can you extend the range to please more people? Can you narrow the range and reduce the price? Can you redesign the packaging to make it more attractive? 'Packaging' applies not only to 'selling' businesses. A furniture-removal firm based near my home recently repainted their vans in a bright colour with their name printed boldly across the side. At the same time, their removal men were supplied with T-shirts in the same colour, also printed with the name. They make quite a striking ensemble which people are likely to remember.

The high-street multiples (Boots, Marks & Spencer,

W.H. Smith, etc.) frequently enlarge the size of their sales outlets, both horizontally and vertically, and sometimes more than once. This allows them to show more wares and pack more customers in. Have you any opportunity to do this? Even if you can't enlarge the building, can you rearrange the layout to cope with more customers? Would it help even if you gave the place a lick of paint to freshen it up?

Take a busman's holiday and spend a few hours going round a number of stores in the same line of business as yours. Take a critical look at the sales assistants. Observe their appearance, manner, initial approach to customers and speed of service. Go back to your own business and try to see it through the eyes of a new customer. Be honest with yourself, and see what you can learn from this exercise. Is the general attitude of the sales staff better in any of the stores you visited? Do any of your assistants need a bit of refresher training? Are any quite plainly unsuited to the job?

What incentives do you offer to attract good salespeople? Do you pay more/less/the same as other local businesses? Once engaged, what training do you give them? Is the quality of your goods or service such that they can take a pride in their work? How much supervision do they get?

What on-going incentives do you give your staff to inspire them to keep on doing their best – commission, bonus, profit-sharing, partnership, or what? To what extent do you rely on your own personality and the example you set? What measures do you take to assess the effectiveness of whatever incentives you use?

Increase sales outlets

The second step towards increasing sales volume is to see how you can increase the market for your goods or services. The ideas under this heading tend to need capital and will probably take longer to implement. Is there scope for opening new branches within your existing sales territory? Are suitable premises available and could you raise the money? Have you enough experienced and trustworthy people to staff the new branches, replacing them with new staff at existing locations? How would your competitors react to such a move?

Would any of your competitors be amenable to a takeover offer, e.g. because of age or ill-health? Are they worth taking over? How much would they expect to be paid? Could you find the money or could you arrange a phased payment? Do you want to keep the existing staff or would you rather put in your own people? Does this cause a redundancy problem? What would this add to the cost?

If you feel that your existing sales territory offers little scope for new outlets, what about breaking into new territory? Usually this entails a study of several adjoining territories, assessing the total market in each and how it is distributed among the existing businesses, using the methods described in chapter 3. How do these compare with your existing territory?

Should one or more of these new territories look attractive, then you begin the process of scouting around for new branch premises and/or considering a takeover bid for one of the existing firms. The further away from home you go, the more appealing the takeover may seem, since it saves you the time and cost of building up a new clientele, but don't allow this to cloud your judgement. The further away you go, the less effective your 'grapevine'. Consequently you must do your research that much more thoroughly to guard against unpleasant surprises. Remember too that the further away the new branch is from your base, the more time you will spend travelling and the more money you will spend on telephones and transport. You will also need a higher-calibre branch manager who can operate without close supervision and must be compensated accordingly.

Adopt new selling methods

In theory, selling methods are chosen to suit the type of customer and the class of market. In practice, the dominant factor is often the personality of the entrepreneur who, in the beginning, is often a one-man band. There is nothing wrong with that, provided you are aware of it. After all, unless you feel comfortable with your goods or services, the customers and the method of selling, you are unlikely to be very successful. And you didn't start a business with the object of being unsuccessful!'

Now that your business is established, you probably have some staff and don't have to do everything yourself. So it is time to take a fresh look at selling methods. You may be able to increase sales by adopting new methods to replace or supplement your present methods. If you don't like to use these methods yourself, you can train your staff to do it or hire someone else. Should you decide after all that your present methods are the best, then you will apply them with more confidence.

The most popular selling method for a small business is face to face, direct to the ultimate customer, as in a shop, market stall or delivery van. Its counterpart with a service is where you go round knocking on doors, inviting people to use your service. This method appeals to the extrovert and is particularly appropriate where the goods or services are not in themselves unique and the success of the business depends mainly upon energetic selling.

An alternative method of selling direct to the consumer is by mail order. You may advertise specific items in the press or invite orders from a catalogue, either directly or through a network of agents. Such a venture may be run from your home or factory, which saves the rent of a shop. It may also appeal to entrepreneurs who lack confidence in their ability to sell face to face. Mail order is particularly suited to goods which have some unique quality, where demand is widely scattered, or where your business is primarily manufacturing rather than selling.

There are still other methods such as: renting a small space within a store where your goods are displayed and sold by your employee (shop within a shop); placing goods in a shop for sale on commission; door-to-door sales representatives (e.g. Kleen-E-Ze brushes); part-time sales representatives (e.g. Avon cosmetics); household parties at which goods are demonstrated (e.g. Tupperware).

Manufacturing concerns frequently sell their products not to consumers but to wholesalers or retailers. This enables them to sell in large batches to a limited number of outlets, the lower selling price being offset by reduced selling expenses. Goods can also be sold in large batches to company or public-sector buyers, or you can submit tenders for goods made to the buyer's specifications. A recent and growing trend is to supply your own goods made up in 'own-brand' packaging for the supermarket chains. Finally, you may use independent agents to sell your products on a commission basis.

Consider each of the above selling methods in turn, and any others you can think of, keeping a very open mind. For instance, you may have to change your class of market and/or type of customer to enable you to employ some new method. Don't just dismiss this – think it through. Would it mean a radically different product or just a change of packaging? Have you got the manufactur-ing/storage capacity required? Could you sub-contract all or part of the extra work? Could your existing suppliers produce what you need?

Should any of these ideas look encouraging, you must consider what effect they would have on your personal workload, both during transition and on a long-term basis. Are any of your staff sufficiently promising to be put in charge of the new activity? Finally, would the new selling method have any repercussions on your existing operation?

Franchising

During the past decade, there has been a considerable growth in *franchising* as a means of enhancing one's prospects of success in starting a new business, albeit at a price. Indeed, the British Franchise Association claims that the small businessman has seven times the chance of success with a reputable franchise, compared with going it alone. This and other aspects of franchising are discussed in some detail in chapter 19.

Sales promotion

If you are going to open a new branch, try a new selling method or make any other change in your business, people won't know unless you tell them. To do this effectively, you need a well-planned *sales-promotion campaign*. This is something quite different from the so-called 'sales promotion' which many businesses do on a routine basis. The latter is often just a glorified name for regular weekly advertising in the local and trade press, backed up by the occasional 'special offer' or a seasonal 'sale'.

If you look at the adverts of many local businesses, you can see how they have got into a rut. They jog along, doing quite nicely; they've already got their circle of regular customers. The owners of these businesses must wonder sometimes whether their advertising does any good, but they are afraid to stop as long as their competitors keep it up. This is why you can seize upon the change in your business as a glorious opportunity. *You* don't have to jog along, you can do something different, *make an impact*, which is what sales promotion is all about.

It is not enough just to make an impact, however; the impact must be effective in the context of your business. Planning a sales-promotion campaign is a staged operation, of which the first step is to define the *target* at which your promotion will be aimed. With the image of the type of customer you have chosen firmly in your mind, can you identify a sector which contains a high proportion of potential customers? Are business customers most likely to be found in organizations of a particular type, size, industrial sector or geographical area? Can your 'typical' individual customer be described in terms of age, sex, social class, occupational group, etc.? The more closely you can define your target, the more effective your campaign will be.

What is the *message* you want to convey to your target? It is not enough just to make them aware of your product or service, you must also make them want to buy it. Look at it through their eyes. Does it make them feel good? Does it provide an easier or better way of doing something? Does it enable them to do something they couldn't do before? Does it allow them to avoid doing something they dislike?

Even if they want what you offer, why should they buy it from you and not your competitor? Is yours better, or cheaper, or in some way unique? What action should they take if they want to buy from you? You must condense all of the above into two or three clear and concise sentences to form your message. Have you any ideas about how some or all of the message can be conveyed by non-verbal methods?

What are the best means of communicating your message to your target? In short, which *media* should you use? In recent years, 'media' has come to be regarded as meaning press, TV and radio, but this is too narrow a view for our purpose. You must also consider other media, e.g. posters; cinema; leaflets (distributed door-to-door or inserted in magazines); bus, train and tube advertising; trade directories; Yellow Pages; and any others you can think of, even way-out ones like hot-air balloons.

Prepare a shortlist of those which seem appropriate and compare them in terms of: coverage of target; suitability for the message; probable effectiveness; cost. Unless you are experienced in this field, you will probably need the help of an advertising agent in assessing these. Then choose the package which seems to give the best overall results for your budget. Incidentally, this should not be charged to your normal advertising or sales-promotion budget but to the start-up cost of the new operation.

Before going into action, you must decide upon *timing*. Is all of the money you budgeted available at the start or does cash flow restrict spending at certain times? Should you make a big splash at the start or run a sustained campaign? Once again, the advice of a good advertising agent is invaluable, but remember that he may be biased towards spending in certain ways.

In addition to the above, there are many varieties of *promotional scheme* such as: give-aways or big discounts on the opening day; an opening ceremony conducted by a well-known person; providing a treat for local children, pensioners or hospital inmates. All of these will cost you money but they are likely to get you some free publicity and, perhaps, some long-term goodwill in the community. Are they worth doing? Such ideas are not usually susceptible to purely financial calculation, so it is partly a hunch decision.

HOMEWORK – CHAPTER 6

6-1. Compare the prices of a few key products/services with those of your main competitors within your sales territory. What do you think would happen if you increased your prices by (a) 5 per cent, (b) 10 per cent.

6-2. Study the sales figures for the last 12 months for total sales and such breakdowns as you have been able to produce (Homework 2-1, 2-2, 2-3, 2-6). What is the total monthly sales target you would like to achieve in 12 months' time? In which sector of your customers would you aim to get the biggest increase?

6-3. Is this sales growth greater than the expected market growth (cf chapter 3)? If so, at whose expense will you make this extra growth?

6-4. After studying your existing business, what action do you intend to take to increase sales? Will this be sufficient to achieve your sales target for next year (cf 6-2)?

6-5. If you don't expect to achieve your sales target through existing sales outlets alone, what action are you considering: (a) opening new branch(es)? (b) making a takeover offer? (c) to whom?

6-6. Review your selling methods in the light of the

alternatives available. Which of these seem practicable for your business? Do you propose to try any new selling methods?

6-7. Do any of the new activities or changes in your method justify setting up a sales promotion campaign? How would you propose to do this? Will you include a sales promotion scheme?

6-8. Take a critical look at your present sales promotion activities. Can you increase their effectiveness?

CHAPTER 7

Increasing your Capacity

The early part of my industrial career coincided with the immediate post-war years. There were shortages of just about everything and demand was way above the nominal capacity of the plant which had survived wartime damage. From this experience, I learned that coping with shortage of capacity can be very tiring and frustrating but also very stimulating. It was very easy to establish good team-work, to call forth and get maximum effort and co-operation. The staff knew that there was a genuine need for everything we could produce. No one was going to work himself – or anyone else – out of a job.

Although when I allow for the exuberance of youth and the rosy glow when looking back, I have to admit that it was a very wearing time. Hours were long and unpredictable and the older staff members must have found it hard-going. Nevertheless, there was none of the fear which often pervades the workplace in the midst of a cost-reduction campaign or when struggling against tough competition. Therefore, I think that the working atmos-phere when 'bottle-neck-busting' is the least unattractive of the various forms of stress to which a business can be exposed. It's always nice to be wanted!

Methods of increasing selling capacity have already been discussed in chapter 6. The purpose of this chapter is to examine ways of increasing capacity in manufacturing, distribution and services.

Manufacturing – diagnosis

The first thing to consider is whether the shortage of capacity is only temporary or whether it is likely to persist in the long term, since this affects one's choice of measures. Generally speaking, one is reluctant to spend any money on equipment to meet a short-term problem. Apart from the question of whether you will earn enough to pay for this equipment, it is often not possible to get additional equipment installed in time to meet the upsurge in demand.

In practice, therefore, the methods of coping with a temporary shortage of capacity are usually limited to one or more of the following measures:

- overtime
- shift-working
- self-employed outworkers
- buying in sub-assemblies
- using sub-contractors for part of the work

There are various ways in which these can be combined to meet a particular set of circumstances, although not all of them may be suitable for your business. Even when the increase in demand is long-term, you may have to adopt one of the above as a temporary measure while you wait for new equipment to be delivered and installed. If all of the increase is due to one new customer, it may be prudent to use a temporary measure for a time before incurring any major expenditure. The new customer may have overestimated the demand for *his* product. Some of the suppliers to de Lorean learned this the hard way.

There are so many different types of manufacturing operations that it is difficult to classify them in any simple way. The commonest classification is to split them into three main types: (a) continuous operation; (b) batch operation; (c) one-off production. Most *continuous operation* is highly capital intensive (e.g. oil refining, car manufacturing) and on a much larger scale than the businesses of most readers of this book. *Batch operation* is often capital intensive, on a more modest scale, and covers a tremendous range of industries: textiles, food processing, printing, furniture, chemicals, engineering components, etc. *One-off production* covers the full gamut of size (and capitalization) from the painter to the shipbuilder.

Another method of classification is into *own production* and *jobbing operation*. In the former, one makes according to one's own design and distributes and sells the product. In the latter, one is carrying out the operation under contract to someone else who supplies the raw materials/components and takes away the product. This is most frequently done as a batch operation but may be on a one-off basis. It will be seen that own production gives more control over some of the factors which influence capacity.

It is very rare for every part of the manufacturing process or equipment to hit the limit at the same capacity. Normally the limit is first reached at one point only, called the *bottle-neck*. This is fortunate because it may not be necessary to increase the capacity of the whole system – just the bottle-neck. Of course, as soon as that bottle-neck is overcome, you may find another very close behind it which must be similarly enlarged. Also, if you run on a batch basis, making successive batches of different products, you may find that the bottle-neck is in a different place for different products.

Finding the bottle-neck

Finding the bottle-neck in a continuous operation is usually a straightforward (but not necessarily easy) technical problem which can be handled by your own staff. If not, you will need to engage a suitable technical consultant to identify the bottle-necks and recommend what should be done. A batch operation may be less straight-forward and the starting point is usually to select a few typical products which between them account for about 60–80 per cent of total operating time.

Take the first product and write down in correct sequence all the steps involved in making that product, including any preparatory steps at the beginning and cleaning up at the end. Note what equipment is used at each step, since we want to find out the capacity of each piece of equipment while making that particular product. In other words, how long is that piece of equipment in use during the making of that batch of product?

Repeat this exercise for each of the other products selected. Now rule a sheet of paper into four vertical columns headed: product, percentage time, first bottle-neck, second bottle-neck. Write down the product which takes most time in column 1 and put the percentage of total time in column 2. Study the sequence for that product and pick out the bottle-neck; put it in column 3. Try also to spot what the next bottle-neck is likely to be and put it in column 4. Repeat this for the other products, in descending order of time. Now decide which bottle-neck(s) need to be tackled.

Not all manufacturers work in the way described above, i.e. turning the whole factory over to one product at a time. Many work in a more flexible manner. They have several products under way at one time and move the material from one piece of equipment to another, letting it 'wait' between each step in production if the desired equipment is already in use. Neither method is inherently superior to the other. It is a matter of 'horses for courses', deciding which is the most suitable method for a particular business. One advantage of the latter method is that it is usually pretty obvious where the bottle-neck lies, and no extensive study is needed to show which equipment always has a waiting list.

Bottle-neck-busting

For reasons already discussed, it is recommended that you first try to meet a shortfall in capacity by temporary means, even when you believe the increase in demand to be long-term. A further reason for doing so is to gain time to experiment and study alternative means of overcoming the bottle-neck. There is often more than one way, with differing advantages and disadvantages. Some experience of temporary measures also provides a cost base against which to compare alternative solutions.

First you should re-examine the short-term measures mentioned above, whether you are using them or not. You may be able to secure more economic rates on a long-term basis. At the same time, study whether it would be possible to overcome the bottle-neck by better motivation of existing staff, for instance: better training; rearranging the work groups and their involvement; providing financial incentives linked to output on individual or team bases; profit sharing. If you decide (reluctantly) that you must increase staff on a permanent basis, you should study the alternatives of at least partial shift-work or more day workers, full-time or part-time.

If you have no option but to install more equipment, try first to get secondhand equipment in good condition, since this is often very reasonably priced. If you have to get new, compare the costs of outright cash purchase, leasing, buying on HP or buying outright with a bank loan. Check also whether there are any grants or subsidies available in your area for such a purpose. Opportunities vary so much from place to place and time to time that it is impossible to generalize, but grants are sometimes very generous.

Sometimes the bottle-neck is simply *space*. You have just run out of floor on which to put work in progress waiting for machine availability, or your staff are almost literally tripping over each other. Alternatively you have nowhere to put the new equipment you need to install. Sometimes this can be overcome by, for example: (a) rearranging the layout to make better use of the floor space; (b) better scheduling of machines to reduce the volume of work in progress; (c) installing vertical racking to provide off-the-floor storage space; (d) shift-working to reduce the number of people on site at one time.

If none of these can solve your problem, you must find more floor space, either by extending your existing workplace or finding a new one. Much of the assistance being given to small businesses today takes the form of help with accommodation. All sorts of bodies are in on the act now: local authorities; local enterprise agencies; development agencies; large companies with spare buildings and a conscience; farmers seeking to make money from unwanted barns. Have a good scout around to see what is on offer in your area.

As a general rule, it is not a good idea for a small manufacturing business to have more than one location. It puts more strain on the owner and supervisory staff who can't be in two places at once. It puts up the bill for rates, lighting and heating, and you may need to have an office and store at each location. But you needn't take my word for it – do your own homework. Unless there is a very strong case for doubling up, you should move the lot to a new location – especially if you can get financial assistance to do so. More information on financial assistance is given in chapter 19.

Distribution capacity

I am assuming in this section that your business is not in motor transport; if it is, you should have enough expertise within the business to cope with capacity problems. I am assuming that you have another sort of business (wholesaling, retailing, manufacturing, etc.) with a distribution which seems unable to cope with its share of the workload.

Drivers work without supervision most of the time and it seems to be almost universal that, over a period of time, cosy little habits creep in and become an established part of their routine. Therefore some improvement in driving productivity is probably attainable in theory, but whether this is enough to solve your problem remains to be seen. Whether it can be achieved in practice is also another matter.

This last point may be connected with how you conduct this study, which will presumably be in keeping with the way you run your business. If you run it in a highly disciplined, authoritarian manner, you will obtain the figures needed, analyze them and issue new instructions. If you run the business with a high degree of staff involvement, you will bring them into the study, get their ideas and jointly discuss what can be done. Both methods can be successful, depending on the kind of business you run and the kind of person you are.

To find out where *vehicle utilization* can be improved, you need to keep a detailed record of each vehicle for a period of, say, four weeks. The records for each vehicle are then summarized under the following headings, listing time and percentage of total time for each:

- *Loading time* – Are there any signs of inadequate loading methods, congestion at loading points, stoppages during loading?

- *Unloading time* (at customers) – Are there any signs of inadequate unloading methods, congestion at unloading points, delays through paperwork, poor discipline of customer staff?
- *Driving* – What is the average driving speed over the four weeks?
- *Authorized breaks* – Do you have fixed times for these?
- *Unauthorized breaks* – This figure may be difficult to obtain.
- *Breakdowns* (on the road) – Total time from first breaking down to arriving at garage.
- *Servicing and repairs* – Time spent working on vehicle.
- *Unaccounted for*.

The above analysis should highlight where there are opportunities to make better use of your vehicles. What it does not show, however, is whether you can improve your *vehicle routing*, i.e. the daily plan of where each vehicle should go. In many businesses this is made up, not by the drivers, but by someone in the office who may or may not have any driving experience.

Get a large sheet of cork or similar material and paste on to it a cheap road map such as garages sell. If necessary, you may have to fit together more than one sheet. Stick a map pin in to locate each customer, using a colour code if you have different types of vehicle. With a piece of string running from pin to pin you can now trace out each day's route and measure the day's mileage from the total length of string. Do a few random checks against vehicle daily mileage records to see if there has been any unauthorized use of vehicles.

Now you want to see if you can improve *vehicle productivity*, which you can measure in ton-miles per day or sales per day, whichever suits your business best. This means turning the improvement you made from your vehicle utilization study into additional deliveries each day. With your map and piece of string you can quickly experiment with alternative routes, checking the promising ones by working out the timed daily schedule to ensure you don't exceed the legal limits on driving times.

At the end of this you should have some more efficient routes, which use fewer vehicle days. You can then utilize the spare days of the vehicle fleet in the way which suits you best; for instance: reducing your use of contract vehicles; disposing of your oldest vehicle or laying it up for emergency use only; better servicing of vehicles; taking on more work.

On the other hand, conducting these studies – or just thinking about it – may cause you to feel that distribution is too remote from your main business to justify spending so much management effort on it. You may decide to contract out the whole job of distribution – many firms do today, even some large ones. But if you have done some of the above studies, you will be in a much stronger position when you come to negotiate with an outside contractor.

A number of other aspects of distribution are covered in chapter 13.

Service capacity

First, may I repeat the point that the division between the three main types of business – selling, making, service – is often unclear and many of the investigation methods described above can be applied to service businesses. That said, I must admit that the range of service businesses is so wide that it is difficult to generalize. Take, for example, car repairs, catering, dry cleaning, instant printing, insurance, travel agents, just to mention a few. What have they in common?

Perhaps the main feature is that they are all dealing directly with the public. Not only the business itself, but many of the staff are dealing directly with the public – and what they say to the customer is legally binding on the business. The customer, therefore, gets his first impression of the business from a face-to-face encounter with what is often a relatively low-paid member of the staff. This puts a high premium on selecting the right staff for the right job and making sure that they are properly trained before they talk to customers. In many businesses the background information keeps changing (e.g. car repairs, building societies) and so it is necessary to maintain a more or less continuous retraining to keep the staff up to date. In such a labour-intensive setting, it might seem that the only way to increase capacity is to increase staff. This is often true but not entirely so. There are ways of increasing the effectiveness of existing staff.

In some businesses (e.g. insurance, travel agents) the assistant spends time finding out what a potential customer wants, explaining what is offered and trying to make a match. Sometimes he succeeds, sometimes he fails. Obviously the real measure of the capacity of that assistant is not the number of potential customers he talks to in a day, but the amount of business he signs up. If you can help the assistant to increase the *conversion* from potential to actual customer, you have increased his capacity.

You can give him training, not just in background information, but in selling. You can provide attractive brochures and visual aids to appeal to the customer. You can provide Prestel, computers and other equipment to find out instantly if what the customer wants is available, and at what price, to help clinch the deal. In other fields you can give the service engineer training and equipment so that he can work more accurately and more quickly.

This saving in man-hours allows you to cope with more business without extra staff.

When so much of the success of the enterprise depends on how assistants behave to customers, it is obviously important that assistants are well motivated. This is part of selection and training of course, but to maintain the right attitudes in the long term many firms find it worthwhile to provide some on-going incentives, such as holiday trips, cash bonuses, or profit-sharing. One of the most effective motivators in small service business is just to call the staff together frequently and tell them how the business is going.

Finding the time

In many small businesses, particularly those dependent upon the personality or artistic skill of the proprietor, the time of the latter can be a serious bottle-neck. In fact, staff may be underemployed at times because the owner hasn't got time to tell them what to do, or he may be so busy running today's business that he hasn't got time to think about tomorrow. Referring back to the discussion in chapter 5 on 'Your own time' and Homework item 5-8, do you think that this might apply to you, at least a little? So how do you go about making more of your own time available?

One of the most effective ways of saving time is to *avoid work*. You might well respond that only a fool does work which needn't be done. I make no comment – just look again at your experimental time-record. Can you say, hand on heart, that every job was absolutely necessary? Ask yourself why each job had to be done? Why that way? Why then? How many jobs were done because you had got into a habit or enjoyed doing them? Can you honestly say there is no scope for skilful pruning?

The next best thing to avoiding a job is to pass it on to an assistant whose time is presumably less valuable than yours – in short to *delegate*. This is very popular management theory, but if you look around you note that many people don't do it in practice. Why not?

Delegation exposes the boss to *risk*. The assistant may not assess the situation correctly, may not decide on the correct thing to do, and may not carry enough weight to get co-operation from others. Another obstacle is *fear*. The assistant may become so good at the job that he gets a better job with your competitor or even starts his own business in competition. Yet a third obstacle is *perfectionism*. It is hard to decide in cold blood to give a job to someone who won't do it as well as you would.

I can only speak here from my own experience. At one stage in my career, circumstances forced me to delegate, and it worked. As a team we were able to keep good control over much more work than I could have done on my own. My assistants matured more rapidly and I got credit for a job well done.

When a task first arises, one often has to improvise a method quickly to get the job done. If the task recurs, this method soon becomes habitual, because it is easier to copy how you did it last time than work out the best way. From time to time, you should step back and examine your own *working methods* as critically as you would those of your assistants.

There are always more tasks to be done than you have time to do. This is usually handled by deciding on *priorities*. Few pay any attention to what Peter Drucker, the well-known business writer, calls *posteriorities*, i.e. the tasks you decide not to do at all. It takes courage to decide to ignore something – but why carry an item for weeks at the bottom of your list before you scrap it? Why not save time by deciding at the start not to put it on your list?

Many problems can be avoided, or at least lessened, by *thinking ahead*. Lack of planning may cause confusion, frequent changes of instruction and duplication of effort, all of which are great time-wasters. Time for thinking doesn't just happen – it has to be made by the methods described above.

HOMEWORK – CHAPTER 7

7-1. Have you got a manufacturing operation? If so, is it mainly: (a) continuous; (b) batch; (c) one-off? Is it own production or jobbing operation?

7-2. What are the bottle-necks in your manufacturing operation? Are any of the temporary measures suggested for increasing capacity appropriate? Have you tried any? If it is necessary to increase your capacity long-term, how do you propose to do it?

7-3. Do you have a distribution-capacity problem? If so, make a vehicle-utilization analysis for each vehicle. Does this pinpoint the problem area and suggest a solution? Have you checked on your vehicle routing and vehicle productivity?

7-4. In spite of (or because of) the above studies, are you now considering putting your distribution out to contract? What do you think would be a fair price to pay for this? What is the maximum price which would still be worthwhile? What would you do about your present drivers?

7-5. Do you have a service-business capacity problem? Could any of the ideas discussed in chapters 6 and 7 be applied to your business? Which ones seem best suited to your situation? Do these still leave part of the problem unsolved? What will you do?

7-6. Is your own time a bottle-neck to the further growth of the business? Will the suggested methods of time-saving overcome this bottle-neck? If not, what do you propose to do?

CHAPTER 8

New Products or Services

Most new businesses confine themselves to a limited range of activities during their early years – and wisely so. Once the business is established and growing steadily, the owner usually extends the range cautiously, keeping close to the initial activities and watching carefully the response of his customers. But there may come a time when he begins to feel he could boost the growth rate markedly by starting a new activity. Of course the risk is much greater than cautiously edging sideways but, if successful, the reward will also be much greater.

If you are thinking along these lines, you may already have a specific new product or service in mind. If not, there are several ways of getting ideas. For instance, you can do a brainstorming exercise, as described in chapter 5, either alone or jointly with family, friends or staff. You can go on a tour of similar businesses, away from your area, to see what new products or services they offer. You can make a close study of the trade press to see what the latest developments are.

One of the best ways is to make a systematic examination of your existing business to see what opportunities there are (e.g. spare capacity, strong points, special skills, etc.) that you can build on. The purpose of this chapter is to show how such an examination can be made and to discuss the factors which should be considered when assessing proposals for new products or services.

Manufacturing opportunities

In many manufacturing plants, not all the equipment is equally loaded. Consequently, even when running at full capacity on existing products, some equipment may have spare capacity. Is there anything you could make using the slack equipment only? Could you get contract work as a sideline to fill up spare capacity? Have you spare space in which you could install new equipment to make products you can't make at present?

What products do your customers buy from other suppliers at present? Could you make any of them at competitive prices? If not, what equipment would you need to do so? Have you room for it? If you made more than your present customers want, could you find additional customers to buy the rest? Could you get a trial batch made to test the market?

Have you any ideas for products which could be made by you, even if existing customers are not interested? Can you make some prototypes to show potential customers? What is the minimum production quantity you could make economically? How would you break into the new markets? Have you or your staff any special skills which are not fully utilized with the existing products?

Selling opportunities

A selling business often has a lot of flexibility in the volume of turnover it can handle at a given location. It can change from slow-moving to fast-moving merchandise; it can change the layout to provide more customer space and less storage; it can change from counter-service to self-service. Consequently it is difficult to say exactly what the maximum capacity of a specific sales location is. (This uncertainty does not of course apply to a high-street retailer with a fixed pattern of merchandise and standard layout.) Nevertheless, when customers stop at the door and turn away, rather than face the crowd within, you'll know that you have gone too far.

On the other hand, if you always appear to have a lot of space in the store, you should consider how this can best be used. A cafeteria is far from an original idea but the facilities available in a particular town or district vary a lot as people enter and leave the catering business. Therefore in any place there are opportunities from time to time. It does not involve much work to make a quick survey of the facilities available in your area and how adequate they are – just check the lengths of the queues at coffee, lunch and teatime. If the need seems to be there, it may be worth costing the project. If you don't want to run it yourself, you can always put it out to tender.

If you can't think of something to sell yourself, you can rent out space to a 'shop-within-a-shop'. This is no longer restricted to cosmetic supplies; there are now many trades keen to use this facility, e.g. optician, travel agent, building society, heel bar. By a suitable choice of trade, they can bring customers to you as well as you to them.

One way of getting ideas for expanding your own business is to get together with your advertising agent and plan a sales-promotion campaign. This should be of the type involving a competition which requires the contestant to hand in a leaflet which includes a question about new products they would like you to sell. Leaflets can be handed out at the store or pushed through letter boxes in the neighbourhood.

If your business is fairly ordinary in terms of its range of goods, you should try to develop some special sideline. No matter how efficiently you run an ordinary business, that's all it remains. So if you are introducing a new product, let it be something special. A special line will bring customers from a much greater distance (or even by mail), besides giving a bit of punch to your advertising.

Service opportunities

As the owner of an established service business, one of your most valuable resources is your list of customers. If properly looked after, this produces not only the bread and butter of repeat business, but the jam from new services. Think about the people who use your service – what else have they got in common? Perhaps this can best be illustrated by the examples of Bert and John.

> 'I'm Bert and I run a home-tuning service. After about three years I found my turnover was levelling off. My customers are mostly regulars or people recommended by them. Various advertising ploys didn't make much difference so I concluded that I'd reached market saturation. I thought about my customers and decided that what they had in common was that they were car owners who wanted their cars well looked after but for various reasons they preferred the work to be done at their home. I wrote to them all and offered to do routine *servicing* at their home, with a discount if they combined it with home tuning. It worked. I got quite a bit of new business – even a few new customers.'

> 'I'm John. I started a carpet-cleaning service a few years ago but soon discovered that there wasn't enough money in carpets alone. I extended it to curtains, then to upholstered furniture, and now I offer a full-blooded spring-cleaning service for those who want it – washing down the walls and the lot. It's a full spectrum, the customer chooses how much he wants done and I offer a fixed-price contract for the package.'

If you look around, you will see many examples of service businesses using their existing facilities to provide new services. For instance, I used to think my milkman was a man who sold milk. He thought so too until he realized that what he was really doing was providing a daily delivery service to households. When looked at in this way, there was no reason to confine his delivery service to milk. Now he doesn't – he also delivers cream, yoghurt, fruit juices, soft drinks, bread, eggs, potatoes and even, at times, meat and poultry.

Another example is my local garage owner. He used to do repairs and sell cars as well as petrol, but when the recession bit into car sales, he closed the car showroom and workshop. As the recession eased, the car showroom has been refitted and opened as a shop for travel-related goods. At the same time, the forecourt was changed to self-service, so that the forecourt staff can now run the shop as well.

Complementary sales and service

When looking for ideas for new products or services, a fruitful approach is often to look for something which is commonly associated with your product; for instance: bacon and eggs, petrol and oil, bed and breakfast. I can remember when shoe shops just sold shoes; now they almost invariably sell stockings and tights also.

The same can apply to services also, as the following tale shows:

> 'I'm Duncan and I'm a skilled welder. After a spell of unemployment, during which I did some odd jobs for car mechanics, I started my own business doing car welding repairs. I soon found that I could get more work if I offered a complete body-repair service. I was able to do the panel-beating and grinding after welding myself, but I still had to pass it on to a spray-painter for finishing. This didn't work out too well sometimes, since I guarantee all my jobs. Now I have engaged my own spray-painter so that I can control the job from start to finish.'

Looking at this point from a different angle, does your business follow a seasonal or any other cycle? If so, can you think of any other business which runs on an 'opposed cycle' to level out the total workload? An example which occurs to me dates back to Scotland before the war. In those days, immigrant Italians had a near-monopoly of the ice-cream and the fish-and-chip trade – they were willing to work the very long hours then necessary. It was very common for an Italian family to have an ice-cream shop and a fish-and-chip shop next door to each other, with interconnecting rear premises. Most of the family then worked in whichever shop was busier, depending on the time of year.

What is synergy?

When takeover bids are being made for public companies, a word often bandied about by the bidder is *synergy*. By this he means that the nature of the two companies is such that when they are put together, they will produce more profit than the sum of the two separate companies. To oversimplify, he is saying that two plus two will produce five when joined together, but only four when separate.

Being practical people, readers of this book will not be surprised to learn that in practice this rarely happens. Few takeovers and mergers produce increased profits right away. In fact, few manage to make two plus two total as much as four in their first year of wedded bliss. In part, this is because the bidder tends to underestimate the expenses of such a union: press advertising, bankers' fees, legal expenses, golden handshakes, and the loss of efficiency while companies are being reorganized. In part, it is because he discovers – too late – that the promised synergy does not exist.

You may be wondering what all this has to do with new products or services in your business. The answer is simply that, whether they know the word or not, synergy is the reason many entrepreneurs seize upon to justify a new project. They convince themselves that, with their existing business sharing all the overheads, they will make a killing with the new venture. Unfortunately, experience with such ventures is often much the same as with takeovers and mergers – disillusion.

Synergy is not a myth but its existence (or otherwise) in a particular proposition can only be checked at the nitty-gritty level. The broad-brush approach is not enough. Since this is the typical approach of merchant bankers and the boards of large companies, it explains why so many mergers and takeovers disappoint the participants. The owners of small businesses spend much of their time dealing with the nitty-gritty, and so have less excuse for error. But they can still be carried away, as Edmund's story reveals.

Edmund's cautionary tale

'Last year I had a chain of four baker's shops, supplied from a central bakehouse. I had just lost the contract for a lucrative business supplying a chain of pubs with bread and rolls when one day I got a telephone call from a Jack Tarvin, who described himself as a business-transfer agent, inviting me to lunch. After an excellent lunch, he asked if I were interested in buying a similar business about thirty miles away – three shops and a separate bakehouse.

'The owner was retiring and in recent years had let the business run down. He showed me some figures which indicated that the turnover and net profit were poor by my standards. He left those with me and arranged to pick me up the next day and take me round, I met the owner, an elderly, very dispirited-looking individual. The shops badly needed redecorating, the bakehouse was decrepit and its equipment ready to be scrapped.

'Because of the condition of the business, the asking price was low. I reckoned I could close down the bakehouse, saving quite a bit of cost, and supply the shops from the spare capacity in my own bakehouse. Even allowing for redecorating the shops, it looked an attractive proposition, especially if I could get the turnover per shop up to my own level. My lawyer and accountant saw no snags so I hurriedly concluded the deal before someone else did.

'Then the troubles started. The product mix for the new shops was different from the pub contract and some days I couldn't make enough pastries. One shop needed much more renovation than 'just a lick of paint' – I hadn't had a detailed survey done. By the time my van had delivered to my original shops, it couldn't supply the new shops in time, although it had been able to cope with the pub deliveries, since they were nearer and opened later. So I had to buy a new van. From the beginning I had trouble with staff – low quality and high turnover (as had my predecessor, if I had troubled to ask).

'The real blow, however, was the slow realization that the previous owner hadn't let the shops run down because he was retiring – he'd retired because the shops were running down:

- one was only two miles from a Sainsbury store which had recently expanded and installed an in-store bakery;
- one was in a district mainly dependent for employment on a large engineering company which had gone broke during the recession;
- one was only a mile from a new shopping precinct which included not only two supermarkets but also a hot-bread kitchen, a health-food shop and a branch of my keenest competitor.

'So now I have a business twice as big as a year ago in terms of capital investment and much more than twice the worry. But profits are only three-quarters of what I made last year. And it's all my own fault. When I bought my first shop, I checked everything with a fine toothcomb. I repeated the process with the second, third and fourth shops. There were no surprises after purchase with any of them. Why then didn't I check this latest acquisition equally thoroughly?

'Was it because my rough calculations looked so good, I thought I was now a big business tycoon who could use his judgement and didn't need to do detailed slogging any longer? Was it complacency? Was it pride? Was it greed? I don't know. Nor do I know how this affair will eventually work out. But I do know I'll never skip the nitty-gritty again.'

Wot, no synergy?

One business on its own cannot have synergy. It is only the combination of two (or more) businesses that can produce synergy, with correspondingly better profits than the sum of the original businesses. Synergy can arise in many ways. For instance, if you own a shop and buy another which you run yourself, then the synergy lies in the shop management. If you have several shops supplied from a central warehouse and buy another shop, now supplied from the same warehouse, then the synergy arises in the warehouse service. Supposing you combine two estate agencies, then you would expect to achieve synergy in the advertising, printing and postage.

As you might expect, synergy is more common when you combine two businesses in the same trade. Nevertheless, it can arise with different trades, given favourable circumstances. For example, one can combine an electrical business with a plumbing business and achieve synergy on premises, shop staff and telephones. But it is easier to fool yourself in such a case, when you know much less about one of the businesses.

While the presence of synergy can make a project more attractive, you should not refuse to consider a proposition because it is absent. The important thing is that you do not imagine it is there when it isn't and so overestimate the profit potential. This can lead you into paying too much and thus condemning yourself to long-term low return or even a loss. Always be thorough in your checking and realistic in assessment.

HOMEWORK – CHAPTER 8

8-1. Think over all the ideas you have had in the past for new products and services. Write down all you can remember.

8-2. Carry out the brainstorming exercise, alone or with others, and write down all the ideas which emerge for new products and services.

8-3. Study other businesses, trade press and publications such as *Exchange & Mart*, and write down any ideas these throw up for new products and services.

8-4. Take the section appropriate to your business (manufacturing/selling/service opportunities) and go through it thoroughly, writing down any ideas relevant to your business. Look through the other sections to see if they trigger off any ideas. At this stage, have you any thoughts about changing to a different type of business?

8-5. Look back over the homework you did on chapters 2 and 3. Do you think you might be getting close to market saturation? Do you think you may *need* to develop a new product or service if your business is to grow much more?

8-6. Can you think of anything which goes 'naturally' with your product or service? Could this provide your new opportunity?

8-7. Go back over all the items listed above. Underline those which might provide synergy, subject to more careful checking.

PART 3
How to Reduce Expenditure

CHAPTER 9

Cost-Reduction Programme

No entrepreneur deliberately spends more money than necessary – and yet a cost-reduction programme almost invariably produces results. How come? In a new business, habits are established very quickly and soon become traditions set in concrete. Your first assistant copies how you do things and, in turn, teaches your second assistant the 'correct' way to do things. But sometimes the method you used the first time was the only way you could think of at the time, not necessarily the most cost-effective. Sometimes you knowingly adopt an expensive method because it is the only way to get the job done in time; next time you forget to tell your assistant *not* to do it that way.

Circumstances are always changing in a business, and unless you make a deliberate effort to review your methods, you will find that what was the most economical method when you started may no longer be so. For instance, through lack of cash or storage space in the beginning, you may have bought raw material in small lots. Now your usage has increased, it would be more economical to buy in larger lots. There may be new equipment available which is so much better that you could show a good pay-out on replacing your existing machines.

As your business grows and you take on staff, you will find that some of them are not as cost-conscious as you. Why should they be – it isn't their business. Although you can train them to do things your way, the instinct is lacking and there will be times when they don't think the way you would. As a result, where you would automatically react to new circumstances, they will plod on doing things the way they were taught.

Short, sharp shock

I have experienced quite a number of cost-reduction programmes and have found that a pussy-foot approach to cost reduction is doomed to failure. It seems to be essential to start the campaign with a short, sharp shock. I think this stems from the supreme importance of creating the right psychological atmosphere needed to get the campaign off the ground.

If you go around for months talking about cost reduction before you *do* anything, you create an impression among your staff that it is not very urgent. Some may think that an adequate response on their part is to go around for months giving lip service before *they* start to do anything.

To get effective action you have to jolt everyone out of their normal mental attitudes, get them out of their ruts. You want them to start questioning everything about their job: 'Why am I doing this?' 'Is it essential?' 'What would happen if I stopped doing it?' 'Is there another way which might be cheaper?'

Sometimes entrepreneurs hold back from starting a full-scale cost-reduction campaign because they fear it may have an adverse effect on their credit rating. On the contrary, the bank manager is more likely to be pleased than worried if a customer says he is about to start a cost-reduction campaign. If well planned and carried out, such a campaign can only result in the business becoming financially stronger. He may even be able to suggest, from his broader experience, which aspects of the business are most likely to repay study.

As an example of one way to start a cost-reduction campaign, let us listen to David's story:

'My name is David. I run a wholesale chemicals-blending and packaging business with a staff of 53. I decided the best way to get maximum impact for starting my cost-reduction campaign was to have a meeting of the entire staff. I chose a Monday because my sales manager was in that day, gave the van drivers short runs and told them to be back by 3.30 P.M. I told the rest of the staff after lunch that we would close at 4 P.M. because I wanted a meeting of the entire staff. I then took the works manager (my deputy), office manager and sales manager into my office and explained my plans.

'Once everyone was assembled in the packing shed, I explained that I was starting this campaign because the kitty wasn't growing fast enough to keep up with my expansion plans. Because my aim was growth, there was no question of redundancy. I also reminded them that the faster the profits grew, the faster their annual bonus would grow. I then announced that, to speed the process, the following temporary measures would come into effect immediately:

- *cheques* – normally all cheques would be signed by myself; in my absence they would be signed by the office manager;
- *orders* – all orders for materials, supplies, etc., over £25 must be countersigned by myself; orders over £10 but under £25 must be countersigned by the works manager;
- *contracts* – all contracts must be signed by myself;
- *permanent staff* – no new or replacement staff will be hired until further notice;
- *temporary staff* – all engagement orders must be signed by myself;
- *overtime* – no more overtime to be worked except with the written permission of the works manager or myself.

'I admitted that this was arbitrary and perhaps unreasonable, but until the campaign had gained enough momentum, I was quite prepared to be unreasonable. I also wanted to receive by 10 A.M. each morning figures for the previous 24 hours for gas and electricity consumption, materials consumption, value of orders placed; stocks of chemicals, work in progress and finished products at 8 A.M. that morning. All of the above were intended as short-term measures until they could be replaced by better long-term measures or until study showed they were unnecessary.

'Finally I told them that the long-term study would begin the next day under the guidance of a committee composed of the three managers and myself. Specific projects would be assigned to individuals or small teams. There would be a weekly progress report posted on the notice board and a review of the whole campaign would be presented at a staff meeting in one month.

'The meeting concluded with a lively question-and-answer session which went on long after normal finishing time. Looking back on it, I think the meeting set the right tone to get the campaign off the ground. The only mistake I think I made was in not having some big visual aids to help explain the situation.'

The long haul

How long should the long haul be? Not too long, I feel. There are two reasons for the 'short, sharp shock': one is to jolt people into doing a mental U-turn, the other is to reach the peak of enthusiasm as quickly as possible. Once the peak is reached, however, enthusiasm, starts to wane. It is better to end the investigation with a few projects still to be tidied up than to let it drag on. The law of diminishing returns applies to cost-reduction campaigns just as much as to other activities. I suggest that you start off with a target of presenting a report in one month after which you will wind it up unless there is obviously justification for continuing.

The main factor which decides how long the investigation takes is, of course, how much in the way of resources you assign to it. It may be possible to release people from their normal duties for one month, whereas you just wouldn't consider it for, say, 3 or 6 months. Consequently, by setting a target of one month, it is easier to assign more people to make the target self-fulfilling.

As a very rough rule of thumb, for a business with more than about 50 staff, I prefer a full-time team of three. That is a good number to stimulate brainstorming within the team. They should preferably be young (twenties/thirties) but have been long enough in the business so that between them they have experience of most parts. They should all be somewhat extrovert, able to get people to talk to them, but at least one should be numerate, like playing with figures, and familiar with any computing facilities you may have.

The above is an ideal; you will have to make do with the best you have – and it should be the best! I would not put more than three in the team, even if you have them; the more you have the more easily they get side-tracked.

For a business of less than 50 staff, I suggest one young person, extrovert and numerate, with a reasonably broad knowledge of the business. It should be possible to release one person full-time (how do you manage for holidays?) but, if not, it should be agreed clearly with his superior how the time should be shared, e.g. mornings on the normal job, and all the rest of the time on cost reduction. Whether full- or part-time, the investigator should be able to call upon part-time specialist help as required. It is also helpful to provide an older person (not his superior) as a guide with whom he can discuss problems encountered.

It is essential that you conduct the cost investigation with the same standard of efficiency as you are trying to achieve in the rest of the business. This means that the effort you make investigating a particular cost element should bear some relation to the prospective savings. It also means that there is a minimum annual expenditure below which it is not worth investigating. It is for you to decide this cut-off point, but it will probably be somewhere in the region of £100.

To get the perspective needed to guide your investigations, turn to the operating budget you constructed in Homework item 4-1. Write these items down in a vertical list in 'extended form', e.g. show the details for wage-related costs (NI contributions, luncheon vouchers, etc.) as separate items under the main heading. In another vertical list alongside put the budget expenditure for each item (breaking down the costs to correspond with detailed items), and in a third vertical list alongside put each item as a percentage of the total cost, and then cross off those items which are below the figure you decided as a minimum cut-off point for investigation.

Make a new list of cost elements, starting this time with the biggest item and then proceeding in descending order of size. At the bottom put 'minor items' to represent those crossed off. Put two vertical lists alongside, one for the budget expenditure for each item, and the other for the percentage of total budget. Fill in the expenditure and percentage for 'minor items' which should restore the totals as before.

It would be ideal if we could forecast the percentage saving which each item is likely to produce before doing the investigation, but this is not an ideal world. To be realistic, therefore, make a fourth list alongside and against each item write 'high', 'medium' or 'low' according to your best guess as to whether that item is likely to produce a high-, medium- or low-percentage saving.

Now pick out the first five items you will investigate. This may be the first five items on the list, but if one or more has a 'low' rating you may feel that some of the items a little lower down offer better prospects. It is important that at least one of the first items you choose produces favourable results quickly. Such a success is a great boost to the enthusiasm not only of the investigators but of all the staff. Another aid to maintaining enthusiasm is to publish progress reports at least once a week.

Cost controls

When you launch your cost-reduction campaign you should at the same time start cost controls, as was illustrated by David's experience above. The first controls will be rather arbitrary and their main purpose is to reinforce the 'short, sharp shock'. They will, however, highlight a number of topics for investigation which might never have occurred to you. For instance, you will probably find that your staff have great difficulty in producing one or two controls which seem quite straightforward to you. Has no one been paying attention to this cost element before? Other cost elements may be much higher than you realized.

As your investigation gets under way, you will gradually scrap some of the original controls, because they are unnecessary, or change them into another which is more effective or is easier to compile. It is not enough to reduce costs – you have to keep them reduced. The opening paragraphs of this chapter describe how inefficiencies creep into any business, no matter how efficient it was to start.

The greatest ally of this insidious deterioration is *complacency*, the attitude that 'it couldn't happen in my business'. It happens in every business, because the only way to stop it completely is to spend much more on controls and investigations than you save in improved efficiency. The object of cost reduction, therefore, is to find the right balance, so that with a modest but highly effective effort you achieve the highest practicable savings.

Most firms find that this balance is best achieved by a combination of regular controls (daily/weekly/monthly) and a booster cost-reduction campaign every 2–3 years. The cost controls themselves should be periodically examined (say, six-monthly) to make sure that they are still necessary, effective, and being prepared in the most efficient manner. At the same time, ask yourself whether any new cost elements have arisen which are not covered by controls but should be.

Staff co-operation

Regardless of your management style, the results of your campaign will be limited unless you get positive co-operation from at least some of your staff – passive obedience is not enough. When you ask for information on a particular activity, you can be misled if no one points out that, due to some quirk in the book-keeping system, the nominal figures are incomplete, since some of the costs are recorded elsewhere. Alternatively, the nominal figures may include some costs belonging to a different activity.

Because of the processing time, many businesses use different bases for allocation to a particular month, e.g. manufacturing output (date of completion), sales (invoice date), account received (date of payment). Consequently, the totals for a specific month do not refer to the same articles. You may not be aware of these and similar discrepancies unless they are pointed out to you.

Of course, you cannot treat your staff for this campaign in a manner quite different from your normal behaviour;

that would ring false and probably confuse them. It is doubtful too if you could sustain such artificial behaviour for any length of time. If you are normally on friendly terms with your staff, then no problem arises. But if your normal behaviour is autocratic or reserved, your staff may hesitate to approach you or to volunteer information.

What type of boss are you? Please try to be very honest with yourself in answering this question, because the problem is not very difficult to overcome. You simply have to take the right action – create another channel of information. The obvious way is to use a member of your investigating team. They have been picked because they are good at extracting information from other people. Or else you can use your deputy or some other senior staff-member as your information channel. If you want to collect the maximum useful information during your cost-reduction campaign, the onus rests with you to make it easy for your staff to provide it.

HOMEWORK – CHAPTER 9

9-1. How would you plan to start a cost-reduction campaign in your business? Which senior staff would you involve in planning and running it? What would you say to staff?

9-2. What emergency measures would you introduce in your 'short, sharp shock'? Which initial controls would you set up?

9-3. Which staff would you use for investigations?

9-4. Prepare the new list of cost elements, in order of size, as described in this chapter. Which cost elements look the most fruitful in terms of expenditure and prospects of achieving a reduction?

9-5. What is your usual management style? What measures, if any, would you take to ensure staff co-operation?

CHAPTER 10

Manpower Costs

Before starting any drive to reduce manpower costs, you must be clear in your own mind what your attitude is towards redundancy. If your business is not growing and creating work for more people, then your scope for reducing manpower costs is very limited if you don't reduce numbers. If you hope to achieve it by natural wastage, is the rate of wastage likely to be high enough in the sections of the business where the surplus manpower will arise?

If you rely on voluntary redundancy, can you offer terms attractive enough to be effective, bearing in mind that a new business is unlikely by definition to have anyone with long service? You may therefore be forced to use compulsory redundancy. This is not a pleasant thing to do but it may be necessary for the survival of the business – and the jobs of those kept on.

As soon as it becomes evident that you are studying manpower – and it is hard to conceal this in a small firm – your staff will suspect the reason. If you don't tell them anything, rumours will start and your staff will suspect the worst, so it is better to come into the open at the outset. If you announce that there may be compulsory redundancy, you may get less co-operation in your study. But if you have previously had good staff relations and handle the matter carefully, you should get your desired result. If you announce that there will be no compulsory redundancy, you will probably get better co-operation, but you may have to wait longer to achieve your results.

It is not an easy decision but is nevertheless one which must be taken early.

Peak workloads

In many firms, at least part of the workload is not uniform but is subject to peaks. If the peaks are small and occur often, then this may be handled by the staff working extra hard during the peak and, in turn, being allowed to slack off at non-peak times. If the peaks are great, however, and infrequent, this solution becomes expensive, since most of the time you have more staff than you really need. In effect, your manpower strength is dictated by peak requirements and reducing staff needs at other times may not result in any manpower saving. What can you do about this?

The first approach, obviously, is to try to eliminate or at least reduce the peaks by better planning. For instance, can you advance or postpone other work so that during the peak workload that is all you have to do? Study your working methods during the peak load to see if you can improve labour utilization.

Is there any equipment you could acquire which would reduce the number of men you need? Can you build up semi-finished stocks in advance so that less work has to be done during the peak? If all else fails, is it worth approaching the customer to persuade him to uplift in small batches? Is it worth offering some financial inducement to do so?

As an alternative, or to supplement the reduction in workload, what can you do to make more people available without increasing permanent staff? I assume you are already using as much overtime as is practicable. Can you get any casual, part-time staff (moonlighters, unemployed) for peaks only? Would it help if your staff staggered work hours? Have you any other staff who could be drafted into this section at peak loads? Are there any union demarcation problems? If so, can a solution not be negotiated? If the other staff are less skilled, can the working methods be reorganized to use these less skilled people? Can you engage contractors just at peak times only?

Reduce the workload

If you don't suffer from the peak workload problem, or have overcome it, you can feel less inhibited about reducing the workload. Obviously one of the best ways of reducing manpower is to reduce the workload they have to do. The best place to start this is with *overtime*, because investigation may show that the workload doesn't exist.

If left unchecked, overtime has a habit of creeping up. In many firms, regular overtime is regarded as a way of 'keeping the boys happy'. This became particularly acute during an earlier period when employers conspired with employees to get round wage controls and fill their vacancies. The subsequent recession has largely eliminated this, but there may be pockets where it still occurs, unknown to higher management. Also, weak supervisors often submit to blackmail when told that jobs won't be ready on time unless some overtime is paid.

For this reason, overtime is one of the items which should be included in the 'short, sharp shock'. Once you demonstrate that you investigate thoroughly any request for overtime which is submitted, you'll be surprised at the drop in the number of requests. I suggest that you don't waste time investigating why this has happened – just be grateful that you have achieved a reduction in cost with so little effort.

Meeting the needs of the customer is the prime consideration when running a business. But you can still try to meet these needs with less workload on your part. Indeed, if you look at articles common today and those made fifty years ago, you will see that in almost every case today's article has a lower '*labour content*'.

This effort to reduce labour content is a continuous one which your competitors will keep up whether you do or not. There are also customers who will want the price to keep coming down and some of them, at least, will accept a lower standard of product or service if it is cheaper. If you choose to maintain your standard that is a challenge that you accept. But you may be at a disadvantage compared with some of your competitors, depending upon your type of business and class of market.

The first thing to look at is your *product design* (if manufacturing), *type of goods sold* (if selling) or *nature of service*. Can the design concept be changed in any way which will reduce your workload? Can you change the starting materials or components to reduce the amount of subsequent work needed? Can you change the finish, or packaging, or the type of delivery service given?

The next item for study is *working methods*. If you have changed the design or concept, does this give you an opportunity to adopt more efficient methods? Even if your end-products or services are unchanged, you have gained a lot of experience since you started your business. If you were starting from scratch to make the same products, would you do it the same way? There may be new materials or tools which have come on the market in recent years. Can any of them be used to streamline your methods? Talk to your production/sales/service staff, the ones who actually do the work on the shopfloor or face to face with customers. Have they any ideas you can pick up, even if they need to be developed?

Can the *layout* of your workplace be changed to reduce manpower needs? Don't think only of the production floor and sales area; what about the stores, office and other 'little rooms'? Has your turnover increased so much since the business started that everywhere is now too congested? Could you take down some walls or partitions to make access easier? Can you extend your building?

Even if you still have enough space, has experience pointed out changes you could make to streamline the movement of people and things? Could the traffic floor in your yard be improved so that you could speed up loading and unloading? Could a better layout help to smooth some of the fluctuations in workload?

When you started your business, you probably installed all the *labour-saving equipment* you could afford. Now you may have more cash available or at least your credit rating has improved enough for you to borrow more to buy or lease more equipment. So what use are you going to make of this opportunity? Is there any equipment you could install which would show a good payback in manpower saving? Could you perhaps remove one or two bottle-necks at the same time?

Improve work efficiency

One of the greatest time-wasters is *job inflexibility*, when a man carries out a job up to a certain point. Then he sits and waits while another man is sent for to remove the nut or do whatever other job the first man is unable, unwilling or not allowed to do. Fortunately it is no longer so common to see 'demarcation disputes' in the headlines, but the problem is still widespread at all levels of our society, from cabinet ministers to fitters. Perhaps this is closely linked to one of our basic psychological needs, which the late Robert Ardrey called the 'territorial imperative'. Nevertheless, it is possible in practice to reduce the problem to negligible proportions.

The easiest way to get full *staff flexibility* is to set the scene for it right at the start. Ideally, one should recruit only staff who can do any of the jobs needing to be done and train them to do them all. In the real world you can't always do this, not least because when you are starting a new business you can't foresee all the jobs that will arise. Also, a new business may not have all that much choice as regards recruits. What you *can* do is to select recruits with a flexible outlook, who are 'willing to have a go' at anything which arises.

The personnel policy you adopt at the outset can also help – or hinder – the achievement of flexibility. You should adopt one with as little in-built demarcation as possible. For example, it helps if you avoid separate 'staff' and 'labour' with different hours of work, canteens, pensions and holiday conditions; separate entrances and time clocks for labour; weekly wage packets and monthly salary cheques.

You should also avoid elaborate hierarchical wage and salary scales with their associated 'perks'. Obviously not everyone is paid the same, but any firm with up to a few hundred staff can manage quite adequately with four or five salary groups which allow a certain amount of over-lap. Perhaps you don't agree with some or all of the above. Well, it's your business and you can run it how you like, but the less demarcation you create in the climate of the business, the easier you'll find it to reduce demarcation on the job. At one time I worked in a plant which did all of the above. My abiding memory of that plant was that never once did I hear anyone say, 'That's not my job.' That plant also had 20 per cent fewer staff than any others of the same capacity.

The advantages of staff flexibility show up not only in

the absence of demarcation disputes. I have found that if staff are responsible for overhauling machines as well as running them, the machines run more smoothly and for longer between overhauls, because of the greater care they receive. There is also better teamwork; the man whose work is running well will help out his colleague who is in difficulty.

This last point shows up too in selling businesses. Staff in a slack department will move over to help in a busy one, without being asked. They will go to the stock room to get something for a colleague who is serving a customer. In an office, too, where the workload for individuals can fluctuate widely from day to day and hour to hour, there is much helping out. Not only does this mutual assistance reduce the total manpower needed to run the business, but it is very advantageous when someone is ill or on holiday to have an experienced and willing substitute.

As I said above, the easiest way to get full staff flexibility is to set the scene at the start. But you are not at the start any longer. Indeed, you may be thinking of ways of reducing staff at the moment, rather than taking on more. So what can you do? First, make up your mind how far you want to go along the road to equalizing conditions for staff and labour. Work out how much it would cost (it may be less than you think) and how you will deal with the transition. Although some may profess disinterest, many 'labour' employees would like very much to be treated as 'staff'. This gives you something to bargain with if you are trying to get their agreement to something else, e.g. more flexibility by removal of job demarcation. If there is a union involved this may cause complications since, even if their members are enthusiastic to accept staff status, to the union it means loss of members. In the end, you may have to sign an individual contract with each employee, over the head of the union.

Your existing staff may also be less than enthusiastic, although they may be too afraid of being called snobbish if they say anything. If they have a union or staff association, the approach is likely to be made through this body. If not, don't assume that silence means acquiescence. They are losing an admission of superiority and apparently getting nothing in return. You may find it useful to give each a one-off, individual bonus or revise the salary scales or do something to make them feel they have been adequately compensated.

In the long run, one of the most influential factors in improving work efficiency is *recruitment* and *training*. In an established business, however, it may well be a long run if you recruit only infrequently. Make sure that those you recruit are up to standard and that they have the flexibility described above. Don't rely only on your own judgement if any special knowledge or skills are required; get one of your senior staff in that line to vet the applicant. Check too whether they have any other skills which might be useful in future.

Training, on the other hand, is a continuous process for existing staff, with the initial training of new staff a minor but important role. Many small businesses think training is a luxury they can do without. If they are thinking of large training centres, lectures, syndicate discussions, video and film shows, they are probably right. But a lot of training can be done on a shoestring by a good part-time trainer with limited facilities.

It is not the facilities that are important but the organization. What matters is setting up the right training programme for the needs of each individual, choosing the right trainer for each part of the programme (rarely the training organizer) and following up its effectiveness. It is a planned 'sitting next to Nellie', with a careful choice of the right Nellie for each stage. The object is to improve the working efficiency of each trainee for the mutual benefit of trainee and firm.

HOMEWORK – CHAPTER 10

10-1. Have you decided that you need to reduce numbers? If so, what method will you use to achieve this – natural wastage, voluntary redundancy, compulsory redundancy?

10-2. Do you suffer from peak workloads? If so, how do you propose to reduce the peak? Do you expect to be completely successful?

10-3. How much overtime do you work at present? What do you think would be a reasonable level?

10-4. How do you propose to reduce the workload?

10-5. Do you suffer from staff inflexibility? If so, how do you propose to overcome this?

10-6. Do you think your existing level of training is adequate? Do you propose to do anything about it? What?

CHAPTER 11

Cost of Supplies

In chapter 5 I said that, broadly speaking, there are three main types of supplies: consumable materials (e.g. stationery, lubricants, cleaning materials); raw materials and components; goods for resale. In the homework for that chapter you worked out the annual expenditure on each of these and expressed it as a percentage of total expenditure. This gives you a sense of proportion and guidelines as to whether or not to investigate any in detail and, if so, how much effort to put into it.

The object of this chapter is to examine the process of obtaining supplies and what you do with them once you get them. This will reveal that there is more to the cost of supplies than just the purchase price. It should enable you to work out the total cost of supplies in your business and indicate where you may have opportunities for cutting your costs.

Choosing suppliers

When a new business is starting, the owner often has little choice of supplier. Few if any will offer credit terms to an unknown; his order quantity is too small for a frequent delivery service, and those willing to supply him may not be the most reliable. Things are now different. You have demonstrated your ability to survive and, I hope, pay your bills on time. Even if the major suppliers are not yet queuing at your door, there should at least be some element of choice open to you.

How will you exercise that choice? From your experience and from talking to other entrepreneurs, you should have a good idea which suppliers will meet your standards for quality and reliability. But there is another question which you may find more difficult to decide: should you go for *single* or *multiple sourcing*? In an effort to reduce their costs at one stage, the car manufacturers went for single sourcing, i.e. only one supplier for a particular component. This gave them considerable leverage in negotiating terms with that supplier. After a prolonged series of strikes, when some suppliers were strikebound while others were not, they changed to multiple sourcing, i.e. at least two suppliers for every component. The theory was that what they now lost on unit cost they gained in security of supply.

You may face the same problem of potential disruption due to strikes hitting your suppliers and must decide whether to combine as many orders as possible for one supplier or not. You will be choosing between cheaper supplies as a result of better discount (or easier credit terms) and more reliable supplies. The choice cannot be sensibly made without knowing how to calculate the value of the various discounts and credit terms and this is the subject to look at next.

In each of the following examples, I have used the same simple figures to make the calculations easy to follow, viz. average monthly purchases £2,000, average interest rate for overdraft 15 per cent.

CASE I – SPOT CASH

This is the base case. Since you pay cash when supplies are delivered, your average monthly payment is £2,000 and there is no interest saving.

CASE 2 – NORMAL MONTHLY CREDIT

This case represents fairly typical credit terms. It is assumed that supplies are received throughout the month and a statement is submitted at the end of the month. Payment is due at the end of the following month. Taking the mid-point of the month as the average date for delivery, in effect you pay for your supplies 1½ months after delivery.

Monthly payment = £2,000
Interest saving = £2,000 × 15/100 × 1.5/12 = £37.50

CASE 3 – DISCOUNT FOR EARLY PAYMENT

Practices vary quite a bit in different trades, so this may not be typical of yours, but the method of calculation can be adapted to your needs. It is assumed that you are offered a discount of 2 per cent for payment within 14 days of invoice date, i.e. approximately ½ month after delivery.

Monthly payment = £2,000 − (£2,000 × 2/100) = £2,000 − £40 = £1,960
Interest saving = £2,000 × 15/100 × 0.5/12 = £12.50

CASE 4 – DISCOUNT FOR BULK DELIVERY

Once again practices vary in different trades but you should be able to adapt the calculation method to your needs. It is assumed that you are offered a discount of 5 per cent for delivery in lots of £5,000, with payment one month after date of delivery.

Payment = £5,000 − (£5,000 × 5/100) = £5,000 − £250 = £4,750
Interest saving = £5,000 × 15/100 × 1/12 = £62.50

After one month, you pay £4,750. But you would only

pay £2,000 under the base case, so there is an outstanding overdraft of £2,750 − £62.50 = £2,687 for which interest has to be paid during the second month.

Interest payable = £2,687.50 × 15/100 × 1/12 = £33.59

At the end of the second month, you would again pay £2,000 under the base case, so the outstanding overdraft is now £2,687.50 − £2,000 + £33.59 = £721.09. Interest on this sum is due for ½ month only.

Interest payable = £721.09 × 15/100 × 0.5/12 = £4.51

The above calculations cover a period of 2½ months, so to make them comparable with the other cases, they must be divided by 2.5.

Payment = £4,750 ÷ 2.5 = £1,900

Net interest saving = £(62.5 − 33.59 − 4.51) ÷ 2.5 = £9.76

Summarizing the above:

	monthly payment	interest saving	net total	per cent reduction
Case 1	2,000	—	2,000.00	—
Case 2	2,000	37.50	1,962.50	1.9
Case 3	1,960	12.50	1,947.50	2.6
Case 4	1,900	9.84	1,890.16	5.5

According to the above calculations, the bulk delivery discount looks the 'best buy'. However, I must emphasize the importance of repeating the calculations with your own figures, since circumstances can alter cases quite drastically. There are other factors to be considered in addition to the above calculations which are discussed more fully later in the chapter. There are more sophisticated ways of doing the calculations which may give slightly different figures, but considering the way order quantities and overdraft interest rates vary, I don't really think the extra work is justified.

Buying

In the previous section, I showed how to compare various types of discount, etc., to bring all the prices to a common base for comparison. This presupposes that the basic price of supplies is the same from all suppliers.

This is often not the case, so a correction must be applied to the basic price. This may be complicated if you buy a number of articles and if suppliers are cheaper for some articles and dearer for others.

In such a case, you'll have to adopt the device used by statisticians when trying to compare the cost of living in different countries. You construct a *shopping basket* consisting of the articles you buy most often. Obviously you haven't got the resources of the government statistical service, so you must keep it simple. Pick the smallest number of articles which will add up to 80–90 per cent of total supplies expenditure. If this number is more than 10, then pick the 10 biggest and accept a less complete coverage.

List the 10 (or less) articles which you buy most in sequence, putting the biggest at the top. Put another column alongside, listing against each article the annual quantity purchased. Put a third column alongside, listing against each article the price charged by one of the suppliers. In a fourth column, put against each article the annual cost of that article from that supplier (i.e. col. 2 × col. 3). Total columns 2 and 4 and divide the total of 4 by that of 2 to give the weighted average price per article for that supplier. Repeat the process for each of the other suppliers.

Price is not the only consideration, of course; quality also matters. But quality is not always easy to assess in the way it affects you. Where the yield of final output is directly related to quality of input, as for example in a chemical feedstock, you may be able to calculate a financial relationship. In many cases it is not so simple and you must try to find a link similar to the following examples:

- percentage of rejects in final product
- wear on equipment
- customer complaints
- reduced production rate
- less pleasant working conditions

Buying a higher-quality material is not the only way of increasing the yield of final product. In some cases, the yield can be increased by changing process conditions, using different equipment, or employing more skilled staff. This reduces the supplies you need to buy for a given output.

In the example calculated above, it appeared that quite a significant reduction in price might be achieved by buying in larger quantities. There are other costs, however, which must be offset against the discount. First, you may have to install additional facilities for the handling and storage of larger quantities. This in turn will be affected by the mode of delivery. Will the larger quantities be delivered in bulk vehicles instead of bags or drums; on pallets instead of in cartons?

Second, even if you don't need more facilities, you will certainly need more space. Have you got it? Paying out larger sums at less-frequent intervals will cause bigger fluctuations in cash flow. The effect of this on interest has been allowed for in the discount calculations, but can you tolerate the bigger payments? The bigger deliveries will affect not only your cash flow; you will also have to increase your insurance cover. So before you make a final decision on bulk buying you should check the financial and operational implications discussed above.

Storage

Depending on the nature of your business, the cost of *storage facilities* may be a big item in both capital and revenue costs. For instance, you may need large tanks for bulk liquid or solid storage. Moreover, if the material stored is corrosive and/or inflammable, you will probably have to observe strict safety precautions and fire regulations. Your insurance bill too is likely to be high, not only because of the value of the facilities but also because of the risks associated.

Another expensive, if less risky, type of facility is freezer storage. The heavy insulation and freezing machinery puts up the capital cost and freezing is not a cheap operation to run. Although less hazardous than storing corrosive or inflammable material, you may have to insure against loss of contents in the event of the freezing machinery breaking down.

There are some other less obvious storage costs such as *deterioration*. Many materials deteriorate in storage, in anything from days (food) to weeks (magazines) to years (paint). In a few cases there may be ways of slowing down or stopping deterioration but, in general, the only way is by strict control of buying, stock levels, and sequence of selling or use. This last point is particularly important. All unstable materials should be date-stamped on receipt and then sold or used in strict order of receipt to avoid any articles being side-tracked and allowed to deteriorate.

Another less obvious storage cost is *loss*, which can occur in various ways, such as:

- evaporation of volatile liquids
- stock damage
- leakage from valves and equipment
- contamination during handling
- spillage
- pilfering
- short receipts from suppliers
- over-delivering to customers

You may never be able to eliminate losses completely but you can reduce them to a reasonable level by providing *good protection* against the above and other forms of loss. Good protection is necessary in every sense of the word. Stocks must be protected against the weather, against fire, against damage, and against people.

One of the best protections is *good visibility*, but visibility should not be an invitation to anyone to walk in and walk off with material. Goods in the open should be protected with heavy-duty, wire-mesh fencing. Inside buildings it is better to have a lock-fast, caged area rather than a closed room. If this can be within sight of your desk or office, so much the better. Then you can see who enters, what they do there, and what they bring out with them.

Care is needed when handling any valuable materials, and you may find it prudent to restrict this work to your more experienced staff. Any losses through carelessness should result in disciplinary action and any form of pilfering is a case for dismissal. Similarly, the paperwork associated with these materials should be checked frequently and any proven fraud should result in dismissal. In particular, be on guard against collusion between office and materials-handling staff, since this is unlikely to be picked up by routine controls.

HOMEWORK — CHAPTER II

11-1.   Are you now in a strong enough position to approach new suppliers? What might you gain from this?

11-2.   How many suppliers do you use? Add up your total purchases and see what leverage this would give you if all or some of your orders were placed with only one supplier.

11-3.   Work out the cash advantages of discounts against interest saving using the examples given in this chapter. What changes are suggested by the results?

11-4.   What information do you have on quality of supplies? Look back at the quality problems you have experienced — or start to keep a record — to see whether there are 'hidden costs'.

11-5.   What is storage costing you? Are there any cheaper alternative methods?

11-6.   Review the paperwork. What is it supposed to achieve? Does it achieve the purpose? Are controls effective?

CHAPTER 12

Equipment Costs

Charles owned a small financial-services company in Manchester with clients ranging from private individuals to small/medium-sized companies in the main towns and cities of England. One of Charles's problems was delays in sending and receiving contracts and similar documents to and from his clients. Most of the documents concerned were sent quite satisfactorily by first-class post but occasionally he needed to deliver on a same-day basis. This most often occurred on a Friday when, if he could get the document into the client's hands before the close of business, he could tie up the deal before the weekend.

Charles had a telex machine but, while ideal for messages, the telex could not transmit a contract or other legal document. Glancing one day at a business magazine he saw an advertisement for a facsimile transmitter – a machine designed for precisely the purpose in hand. Charles bought the machine for £5,000 and incurred a further cost in installing the necessary additional telephone line. He realized his mistake when it dawned on him that none of his private clients had a facsimile transmitter with which to receive his documents, and only about 5 per cent of his company clients had one. Considerably out of pocket, Charles eventually turned to courier services which almost always met his needs.

Charles's experience illustrates the first rule of equipment selection, which is to ask the following questions:

- will the equipment do what I want it to do?
- how much will it contribute to profit?
- is there any better alternative?

Having answered these questions, and depending on the answers, we can apply the acid test:

- Do we really need it?

No doubt this all sounds obvious, but it is amazing how many purchases of capital equipment are made without checking the facts. Purchases are sometimes made on impulse, sometimes to keep up with the Joneses (especially in the case of computers) or in response to a fast-talking salesman. None of these reasons is good enough, and a more disciplined, analytical approach is necessary.

The following is a check-list of points to watch when deciding whether the equipment will do what is required:

1. Is the design compatible with other equipment already in use? Electronic equipment using disks must allow for interchangeability of disks.

2. Are the manufacturer's quoted speeds achievable in practice? Remember that a quoted speed of, say, 100 pressings per hour can only be achieved as long as work is available and, if work arrives in peaks and troughs, a speed of 200 pressings per hour may be required. Similarly, the quoted speed may depend on the operator, who may not be able to cope with the machine going at full speed for more than, say, 30 minutes.

3. How often will the machine be out of action for routine maintenance or repairs?

4. Is the capacity/capability of the machine suited to all the work likely to be required? – e.g. a multiple wood-working machine will have limits to the widths and thicknesses that it can handle.

5. Will the equipment operate efficiently in severe conditions of temperature and humidity? Something that works well in an office may break down in a foundry.

6. Will the equipment stand up to tampering or other abuse by the general public? Any equipment housed in a place where the public have access is liable to be 'played with'.

Let us now consider the second question: 'How much will the equipment contribute to profit?' The great difficulty here lies in the fact that the value of a machine in terms of the revenue it can earn for the company must be determined, not only in the light of present circumstances, but also in terms of long-term forecasts. We may be quite confident of our expected use of the equipment in the first year or two, but what then? We may have no use at all for the machine in 3 or 4 years' time.

One way round this problem is to take a view on the likely period over which a 'pay-back' can be obtained. Let us take, as an illustration, the relatively simple case of an automatic car-wash:

Purchase and installation cost – £10,000

Gross revenue per customer – 50p

Materials used per customer – 5p

Maintenance costs per month – £20

Other monthly costs, e.g. insurance – £20

Expected number of customers per month (after allowing for repairs and other 'downtime') – 200

On the basis of the above figures the gross revenue per month will be 50p × 200 = £100.

From this figure we must deduct 5p × 200 for materials (£10) and a total of £40 for maintenance, etc., yielding a net revenue of £50 per month.

On this basis the initial purchase and installation cost will be 'paid back' after $^{10,000}/_{50}$ = 200 months – just over 16 years!

Clearly, not only is a period of 16 years far too long to wait, but car owners may not even want the service by then. The self-cleaning car, if someone invents it, will be the end of all car-wash services! If, however, we could confidently forecast 2000 customers a month for our car-wash, then the position is entirely different. The payback period would be reduced to just under one year. This is a much more satisfactory period in the sense that we can see much more reliably what is likely to happen in the way of competition and demand.

Although a fairly simple example, the car-wash calculation illustrates the approach required in evaluating potential equipment. Some calculation is necessary, depending on circumstances, to provide an objective (even if only approximate) idea of the revenue and profit likely to be gained.

Sometimes new or additional equipment will save labour and contribute by reducing wage costs per unit of output. Sometimes quality improvement may be gained to either meet the competition or open up a new market. Whatever the case, no purchase of new equipment should be made unless a *clear* contribution to future profit can be seen.

Similar costings may be required to answer the third question: 'Is there any better alternative?' Not only is it necessary to compare the features and costs of similar equipment offered by other suppliers, but profitable results can be derived from turning the whole subject on its head; going back to square one and asking if there is any other way of achieving the result without buying equipment at all. There is always the chance that one of the following lines of action will be cheaper:

- Sub-contracting all or some of the work
- Re-designing the product so that it can be made using existing equipment
- Adapting existing equipment to enable it to do the work.

Reducing the cost of existing equipment

There is a 'classical' problem which besets all users of machinery, whether it be computers, communications equipment such as telex machines, factory machinery, or even vehicles. This is the problem of what to do when along comes a more modern and more efficient equivalent machine long before the old one has reached the end of its useful life. The businessman must decide whether or not to replace his old but still usable machine with the new alternative.

The reasons against replacement are often quite irrational and are expressed like this:

- 'There is plenty of life left in the present machine; why waste money buying a new one?' (the production manager)
- 'The present machine is not yet written off and has a book value of £x' (the company accountant)
- 'We can't afford more capital expenditure' (a major shareholder)

Providing the new machine *is* more efficient, none of these statements is valid. Firstly, buying a more efficient machine is not likely to be a waste of money as the figures (to be illustrated later) will show. Secondly, keeping the machine until it is written off doesn't bring any money back nor does it provide money for a future purchase. Lastly, you may not be able to afford *not* to make further capital expenditure – especially if competitors are buying the more efficient equipment.

Let us take an example. Suppose a business uses a 3-year-old Magic Lathe which works well and cost £1 per unit of output to run. Along comes a salesman offering the Auto Lathe which, needing no human attention, costs 75p per unit of output to run. We paid £5,000 for our old lathe and the new one is offered at £6,000.

The first step is to calculate how much we will save by using the new machine which completes each unit for 75p. Obviously we would save 25p per unit. If we produce a total of 10,000 units per year we would save 10,000 × 25p = £2,500, and at this rate we would 'get the money back' in just over two years. After that, by using the Auto Lathe, we are making more money than we could have done with the Magic Lathe.

The businessman in this position must swallow his sadness at having to dig into his pocket so soon after the last time and take on the new machine. Keeping the old one until it is written off will not bring the money back but will make him uncompetitive with companies which opted for a new machine – giving them a chance to reduce prices.

Sadly, many of the now-derelict factories in the Midlands were equipped with old machines (some going back to the First World War!) and those businesses went under against the competition of well-equipped German, Japanese and American companies.

Routine controls to save money

Management must go to the trouble of keeping a close eye on a range of practices, however tiresome this may be, to prevent money leaking away. The pressures of dealing with customers, the excitement of the impending stand at the trade exhibition, and the tensions of negotiations with suppliers must not be allowed to detract from attention to the nuts and bolts of the business. Among the more important equipment considerations are:

- *Repair records* – Records of any repairs to equipment should be kept in detail – showing time, duration and nature of the breakdown and the cost of the repairs. This is essential as evidence to be presented against manufacturers' guarantees and, in extreme cases, to claim against them for contraventions of the Sale of Goods Act or other manufacturer liabilities. A good record can make all the difference between adequate compensation (including a free replacement machine in extreme cases) and merely losing time and money. Records should also be scrutinized regularly to see how often breakdowns occur and for what reason. Trouble may be caused by an inadequately trained or careless operator, or by sub-standard raw materials, lubricating fluids and the like. Such causes need to be spotted as soon as possible and attention to the records is the way to do it.

- *Servicing schedules* – Proper servicing and maintenance is essential to make possible continuous and economical production. Failure to carry out proper servicing can not only result in lost production time but also make any claims against the equipment manufacturers difficult or impossible to prosecute. The emphasis should be on preventative servicing, resisting every temptation to delay servicing in order to complete some urgently needed production. There is almost always some urgently needed production in a busy company and the situation can be prolonged until a breakdown occurs – often at the worst possible time. Inspection, servicing and overhaul must be built into the production plan from the outset and not relegated to an 'as and when' activity.

- *Machine utilization* – If machine A makes things for use in machines B and C, then the output of A must balance with the outputs of B and C. It is not always easy to achieve this situation and either:

  (i) Machines B and C are starved of parts, or

(ii) B and C cannot keep up with A and A stands idle for some of the time.

There may, in addition, be other machines very little used.

Records should be kept of utilization and these should be regularly examined to see if cost-saving opportunities are available, e.g. it may be possible to run machine A on a night shift in order to stockpile parts for B and C. Alternatively, if machine A is idle for a significant time, some shift working on B and C may be possible.

Other under-used machines may now be virtually surplus to requirements and could be sold and the work placed outside with a sub-contractor. As a general 'rule of thumb', a utilization of 75 per cent of the working time available should be aimed at, having allowed for maintenance downtime.

Buy, lease or rent?

The differing tax situations between partnerships and limited companies and the variations of tax rules which come and go with governments and Chancellors of the Exchequer make it impossible to lay down hard and fast rules as to the economics of buying, leasing or renting. What is best for one business may not be best for another and what is best in one year may be worst in the next.

Clearly, leasing and renting avoid difficulties in finding capital, but the tax situation needs to be reviewed from time to time and professional guidance sought. It is important to avoid the mistake of thinking that what was a good method last time will be a good method in future. Tax aspects are further examined in chapter 17.

Production planning and machine scheduling

Careful scheduling of machines and the work to be done on them was recommended in chapter 7. Both scheduling and production planning have a positive though indirect impact on equipment costs by ensuring that optimum use is made of existing resources (thus cutting unit production costs) and postponing the time when more money is spent on additional machines.

Production planning involves looking at orders already received, those expected, and also any production for stock. The further one can look ahead the better, but even a few days or a couple of weeks can make the difference between efficient economical working and machines either standing waiting or idle during frequent change-overs.

There are a variety of ways to plan production, ranging from examining a pile of orders and putting them in a priority sequence which takes account of commercial factors as well as production economies, to using a computer to analyse the position regularly. A good compromise is to use a planning board – visible to all – which shows the orders in the pipeline and the expected production dates. A blackboard will do but more convenient is an 8′ × 4′ board marked into days, weeks or months with orders on 'Post-it' notes stuck in the appropriate places. The notes can be moved about as work is completed to show the latest situation at a glance.

HOMEWORK – CHAPTER 12

12-1. Prepare your own check-list of points to watch when deciding whether or not to buy the sort of equipment you are likely to use in your business.

12-2. Do you have a costing system, appropriate to your service or product, to ascertain how much a new acquisition will contribute to profit?

12-3. Review the equipment you have in terms of its *present and future* value to the business.

- Is there anything which should be sold?
- Is there anything which should be replaced?

12-4. Review your control procedures to ensure that:
  - There are adequate records for the purposes of servicing and maintenance.
  - You can see how much a machine is costing you in lost time and/or repair bills.
  - Equipment is being used properly and not mishandled or abused.
  - Utilization of equipment is the best you can make it.
  - There is some effective form of machine scheduling and production planning.

12-5. Review with your tax adviser your policy in respect of buying, leasing or renting equipment and make appropriate changes to your policy for the future.

CHAPTER 13

Distribution Costs

The term 'distribution' covers a wide range of topics including packaging, warehouse design, material-handling systems, and so on. This chapter is concerned with the two main aspects of distribution – transport and storage. These are the two factors which have the most influence on costs and which are fundamental to the degree of customer service that must be provided to beat the competition.

Service companies must also consider distribution as part of their business, even if they have no physically tangible product. As someone once said, 'Distribution is all about putting the product or service where the customer wants it.' It is for this reason that building societies vie with each other for convenient high-street sites, large London law firms have offices abroad, and Lloyds insurance brokers link up with 'producing brokers' in other countries. All of these service businesses place their 'product' within easy reach of the customers, and the cost of doing so must be an integral part of business planning.

The manufacturer, the wholesaler and possibly even the retailer will be more concerned with the transport and storage costs involved in placing their tangible products in customers' hands.

Some alternative considerations

The basic consideration from which all distribution planning is devised is the speed of delivery required. If competition or the nature of the business or product demand a same-day service, then a certain level of cost related to a minimum level of resources (vehicles, etc.) will be unavoidable. If, however, a delivery time of, say, 2 weeks, is entirely acceptable, then resources and costs can be geared accordingly.

The businessman will almost always face a conflict in that while he wants to save money (and service to customers costs money) he must always provide a level of service as good as his competitors. The business that fails on service loses sales. No sales means no profit and, hence, no business.

The 'trick' is to identify clearly and *realistically* the standards necessary and then find the most cost-effective way of meeting the standards. Fortunately there are a number of options open to the cost-conscious entrepreneur.

Be realistic

Nothing is easier, or more dangerous, in business than to allow 'old wives' tales' or emotion to dominate thinking. One of the worst old wives' tales was trotted out by Ralph Waldo Emerson when he said, 'If a man can . . . make a better mousetrap than his neighbour, though he builds his house in the woods, the world will make a beaten path to his door'. This may have been true in earlier days before mass-production, mass-communication and mass-competition. It is unlikely to be true today and cannot be relied on – however good the product.

An example of the 'emotional approach' to distribution is illustrated by the following cautionary tale:

Ian, who jointly owned and managed a small engineering business with his brother, insisted that top priority should be placed on speedy delivery and adopted a 'blind policy' of a maximum 2-day delivery time. He was convinced that this must be a 'good thing'. No expense was spared – including, on one occasion, air-freighting a parcel to the Isle of Man.

The result, apart from higher cost, was only a very limited improvement in service since the total elapsed time from the moment that the customer mailed his order to producing and delivering the product was so great that a day or two saved in delivery made little or no difference *in the mind of the customer*.

Wendy, on the other hand, who made and sold wicker-ware products, lost customers due to *irregular* deliveries. 'I found that the cost of my small van was becoming an increasing burden and every time petrol went up a penny or two I saw my profits eroded. A friend suggested using a public carrier, but I felt that this would be an admission of defeat. Instead I grouped my deliveries together, saving them up until I had a whole vanload. This certainly saved petrol and driving time but I lost a lot of customers who had come to depend on regular deliveries.'

Wendy had failed to distinguish between *fast* delivery and *regular* delivery when thinking about the service her customers wanted. As one of them said to her, 'I am more concerned with reliably knowing when the goods will arrive than how quickly they will arrive.' It should not be forgotten that a dependable delivery service enables customers to cut their stock-holding costs.

Distribution as a 'Positive Force'

Before looking in some detail into ways and means of reducing or saving distribution costs, it is worth considering one more 'conceptual' aspect of the subject.

Most businessmen look upon distribution as an expensive but unavoidable back-up to production and sales. Better results will be achieved by taking the more positive line of thought that distribution should be built into the design of the whole business in order to 'add value' to the product. In other words, look at distribution as part of the design of the product – the part that makes it easy and convenient for the customer to buy. The best possible product that man can devise still needs to be in the right place at the right time and, if it is, gives the business a vital competitive edge.

Moving things

This section could have been headed '*Moving Product*', but we should also consider moving semi-finished goods and raw materials as well as products. It may be convenient (or at times save money) to collect raw materials from suppliers or to take semi-finished products to a sub-contractor. In any event, transport of some kind is needed.

Let us first consider Andrew, whose experience illustrates a number of useful ideas.

'I started a business restoring antiques and making general repairs of furniture. I knew that it would take a long time to develop a clientele and did not want to spend money on a vehicle. I was, in any case, very short of money and had no credit-worthiness to offer to the bank manager.

'Nevertheless, I had to find a way to collect items of furniture from customers, take them to my workshop and return them when the work was completed. I dealt with the problem in the only way open to me by shopping around and finding a van-hire company offering vehicles at a reasonable daily rate. This worked well for some time, especially when I was able to combine two or more trips in one hiring.

'After about a year my business was building up rapidly and I concluded that if I bought a secondhand van I would be more independent. I found an elderly, battered vehicle which was cheap and calculated that even with tax and insurance I would save money over daily hirings if the van lasted six months or more.

'I bought the van and, in fact, it lasted for a year, by which time my cash flow was good enough for me to lease a new van. I still hire other vehicles from time to time when I have an unusually large load. Such loads are infrequent, and it does not pay me to lease a large vehicle as well as the van.'

Lessons from Andrew's experience

Whether he consciously realized it or not, Andrew carried out the first analysis required to determine the type of transport he needed. This was to look at the 'delivery demand' of his business. This demand can be one or more of the following types:

LOCAL	– URGENT	(e.g. fresh-cut flowers)
LOCAL	– NON-URGENT	(e.g. repaired furniture)
LOCAL	– REGULAR	(e.g. supplies to retailers)
LOCAL	– OCCASIONAL	(e.g. deliveries to private individuals)

There can also be combinations of the above such as the delivery of fresh-cut flowers to a retail florist's shop. These will be URGENT and also need to be REGULAR. The same types of delivery demand can be applied to DISTANT deliveries.

Andrew decided that his deliveries were non-urgent and occasional, so hiring a van on an occasional basis would meet his needs and avoid capital expenditure and overheads.

So step 1 is to identify the nature of the delivery demand and decide the cheapest way to meet it.

Some of the alternatives available which avoid capital expenditure are:

- Hired vehicles (self-drive)
- Road carriers
- Rail services, e.g. Red Star
- Mails

Should your product, and the necessary service to customers, suit any of these methods they should be seriously considered. Some of the largest manufacturing companies use common carriers (either exclusively or in combination with their own vehicles) having examined the costs involved.

The basis of your decision will be a costing which compares the charges for outside services with the expense of running your own vehicle. Your own vehicle will incur a number of fixed costs which must be met regardless of the number of journeys you make or miles covered. These fixed costs are:

    Lease or depreciation costs
    Tax
    Insurance
    Garaging

In addition, variable costs will be incurred depending on the mileage covered. These variable costs will include:

    Fuel
    Maintenance and servicing
    Replacement parts (e.g. tyres)
    Washing

If a driver is employed his wages must, in the short to medium term at least, be considered a fixed cost. A driver may of course be able to carry out some of the maintenance and also keep the vehicle clean, but one way or another these items must be paid for.

Let us now consider how a comparison might be made between running a vehicle and hiring one when required. For this purpose I will assume total fixed costs of £1,800 per year. (I am also assuming that the proprietor or one of his staff will do the driving when required so that labour costs are the same in both cases.)

For the purposes of this illustration I am assuming variable costs to be 20p per mile. If journeys work out at one per week, averaging 50 miles per journey, throughout the year, then variable costs for the year will amount to 52 journeys × 50 miles × 20p = £520. The total cost per year will be £1,800 + £520 = £2,320, which works out at $^{2320}/_{50}$ = £46.4 per journey.

If, say, an equivalent vehicle can be hired at £20 per day, convenience apart, it is clearly more economical to hire a vehicle than to buy one. It should be borne in mind that the above illustration simplifies the problem, and in real life allowance must be made for such things as maintenance or repair sessions when your own vehicle will not be available for use.

Another important point to watch is the ratio of delivery costs to the gross profit earned from the goods delivered. Unless the customer will pay the delivery costs then the seller's profit is reduced accordingly.

Having worked out the total cost of an owned or leased vehicle, the businessman can compare this cost with that of any suitable outside delivery service taking into account the number of journeys to be made and the service needs of his customers. Andrew worked out that a cheap secondhand van became worthwhile when his volume of business reached a certain level. He was aided by a low depreciation cost as his capital outlay was very small. When his number of deliveries (closely related to his level of 'sales') reached an even higher level, he could afford the higher cost of a leased van which he also felt was better for his 'image' than the battered vehicle he started with.

Other pros and cons of hiring or owning a vehicle

Apart from costs, the businessman must take various other factors into account when making decisions about vehicles. Among the advantages of having your own vehicle is the fact that, with suitable wording (your name, logo, slogan, telephone number, etc.) your vehicle can act as a mobile advertisement. This can be worth quite a lot in terms of free publicity, providing care is taken in two respects:

• The vehicle must be kept clean and in good condition
Nothing could be worse than your business being associated with a dirty, dented old vehicle with a light or two not working, belching diesel fumes all over other road users. Not only is this likely to attract the interest of the police, but it will irritate others and leave the impression that your business, like your vehicle, is a scruffy, ill-managed operation.

• The vehicle must be courteously driven
Vehicles which jump red lights, are left parked across entranceways, and which are generally driven badly will also attract unfavourable attention. Your driver may not be the most thoughtful and intelligent person on earth, and once he is on the road he is beyond your supervision. Care must be taken to see that your vehicle is properly driven, although you can never be entirely sure.

Roger, a buyer for a pharmaceutical company, was driving home from his office one evening, having just received very similar quotations from two suppliers of packaging materials. He was not certain which offer to accept when, approaching a crossroads on the A40, he saw a lorry emblazoned with the name of one of the two would-be suppliers approaching on the minor road to his left. 'To my astonishment,' said Roger, 'the lorry shot out into the main road and, if I have not braked very hard indeed, would have taken the front off my car.' Roger then added, 'That decided me. I was so annoyed by the behaviour of the lorry that I made up my mind that the suppliers concerned would not be the ones to win the order.'

Roger's reaction was of course an emotional one, and he made a decision which had nothing to do with the merits of the suppliers under consideration. But this *true story* illustrates the fact that decisions are influenced by non-relevant matters and your 'image' could be one of them.

Another advantage of having your own vehicle is the fact that you have a resource at your disposal for emergencies. You may not be able to hire a vehicle at just the moment you need to make an urgent, possibly unexpected, delivery, or to dash to a supplier for badly needed raw materials.

This 'convenience factor' can be very important in some businesses where customer-service demands make the sudden ad hoc delivery important. Meeting the demand can make all the difference between keeping or losing a customer.

Once again, however, a realistic approach to this question is necessary, e.g.

- How often are 'emergency' trips *really* essential?
- Can you *profitably* provide such a service?
- If you frequently run out of supplies, do you need better control of your stocks rather than an expensive vehicle? Are you planning ahead properly?

The non-cash disadvantages of having your own vehicle include a number of 'worry factors', viz.

- Someone must remember to tax and insure the vehicle and take the time to do it

- Maintenance schedules must be adhered to and again someone must keep the records and arrange for work to be done

One of the most irritating discoveries is to find that, at a time when the vehicle is badly needed, it is overdue for servicing. There is a temptation to skip servicing due to the pressing need to make deliveries, and this can go on until the vehicle breaks down (always at the worst possible time) leaving you with no service at all. This is a classic case of 'the urgent taking priority over the important'.

All these worry factors can be handed over to someone else if vehicles are hired. There is an attraction in letting the manager of the hiring company have the sleepless nights.

Another way of looking at the costs

We have already looked at expenses by working out fixed and variable costs and making comparisons of 'cost per mile' and 'cost per journey'. There is a further approach which is helpful when evaluating charges for mail, road carriers and rail as possible alternatives.

These services are often charged on a weight basis, so to obtain a comparison a similar calculation must be made in respect of owned or leased vehicles. This involves working out, as before, the fixed and variable costs, and then applying them to the weight of goods being carried on an average journey. Thus, if your own vehicle carries an average of 5 cwt every time it makes a journey from, say, London to Southampton, the cost per cwt is total journey cost ÷ 5. The cost per cwt quoted by a common carrier may be more or less and hence worth considering or not.

This weight/cost calculation is likely to be most helpful

to businesses where products are sold by weight, e.g. vegetables, chemical products and a variety of dry goods.

Summary

Economies in moving things will only be found when the costs of the alternatives have been worked out. Having made the effort, however, the rewards can be considerable – especially if a truly realistic approach to service, convenience and profit is taken.

Storing things

A cost frequently overlooked or given inadequate attention is that of holding stocks. Although the businessman is well aware of the money he pays out to buy raw materials and other supplies, he can easily overlook the cost of holding them. It is even easier to underestimate the cost of holding semi-finished goods and finished goods.

The cost of storing any item will include what the accountants refer to as 'opportunity cost'. That is the cost of not using the equivalent money in some other form of investment. In other words, one can choose between spending £1,000 on raw materials and, say, putting the money in a building-society account to earn interest. The opportunity cost of holding the stock of raw materials is the interest that would have been earned if the money had been invested in the building society. So long as a stock of anything is held, it must be considered as losing the money which could have been gained by taking the other opportunity.

However, there are few business which can operate with no stocks at all, even if they only comprise office stationery, and many require considerable quantities. The objective should be to keep the quantity to a minimum.

Let us suppose, that a business normally has a stock of raw materials, spare parts, etc., amounting to £20,000 in value. Let us also suppose that the company has borrowed £10,000 at 12 per cent from the bank. If the stocks could be reduced by 50 per cent, what would be gained?

Two opportunities present themselves. Firstly, if the liquidity of the business can be increased by £10,000 as a result of the stock reduction, then the bank loan could be paid off. This would save 12 per cent of £10,000 p.a. = £1,200 p.a. Alternatively, the £10,000 could be invested at, say, 8 per cent to yield £800 p.a.

It is equally likely that the cash could be used in some other way, such as hiring more labour, renovating machinery, an advertising campaign, or whatever else the business needs to expand and, hopefully, become more profitable.

The only possible advantage which can result from overstocking is that the goods held increase in value at a rate greater than the opportunity cost. This does sometimes happen but not very often, and is normally a lucky 'accident'.

The other costs

Apart from the opportunity costs, there are other, more obvious, costs associated with holding stock. These include:

> Warehouse rent and rates
> Insurance
> Obsolescence
> Pilferage and deterioration
> Labour
> Maintenance and repair of buildings

    Heating and lighting (sometimes refrigeration)
All this can add up to a substantial total and applies to all items stored, whether raw materials, goods in process or finished products.

Why store goods at all?

Before looking at ways and means to reduce stock-holding costs, let us consider the purpose behind stock holding in order to be clear about the need. Ideally, a business would receive its raw materials in the morning, make the product and sell it in the afternoon. Sadly, life is rarely so simple.

    There are a variety of reasons for stock holding including the following:

Raw materials	– To keep the production process continuously supplied – avoiding costly idle time
	– To protect against any unexpected shortages of raw materials, e.g. as a result of strikes
Goods in process	– To ensure that one stage of production is not held up when another suffers some delay or calamity
	– The unavoidable build-up resulting from a stage of manufacture being normally and properly completed
Finished products	– To have a stock available to meet orders which arrive in a random fashion
	– To accumulate goods in anticipation of delivery to satisfy a known requirement, e.g. an order already placed for delivery at a specific time in the future

Goods will normally be purchased or manufactured to meet most of the above requirements and it is essential, as a first step, to be clear as to the reason. Having decided the reason for the stock holding it is possible to move on to use one or more techniques for reducing the stock held to a minimum and hence to minimize the costs.

Reducing the quantity and the cost

RAW MATERIALS AND FINISHED PRODUCTS BOUGHT FOR RE-SALE

The key element which determines the necessary minimum stock holding is the speed with which suppliers can deliver and their reliability. If, for example, a supplier is 100 per cent reliable and can deliver in one hour from receiving the order, then virtually no stock will be required at all. It is more likely that delivery will take, say, two weeks, and there is a fair chance that one or two days will be added to that time, coupled with the chance of a short delivery.

The first stage in keeping stock-holding costs down in this unsatisfactory situation is to work out what is termed an Economic Order Quantity (EOQ). For those who are interested there are, in textbooks on the subject of stock holding, some fairly complex mathematics involved in calculating the EOQ. For the purposes of this book, I have taken a simplified version which works well enough in practice.

The easy method is to draw up a table of varying 'order sizes' and to enter a figure for the various costs associated with each. These costs will include:

Opportunity cost, say 10 per cent of the value
Order costs, i.e. the clerical costs involved

Miscellaneous labour, e.g. unloading, carrying, checking

Discount for quantity

This is how they might look in a table for an item costing £5 a carton:

Number of Orders p.a.	1	2	5	10
Size of order (cartons)	1000	500	200	100
Opportunity cost £	100	50	20	10
Order costs £	5	10	25	50
Labour £	20	18	15	12
Discounts £	(50)	(25)	—	—
Total cost	£ 75	£ 53	£ 60	£ 72

It will be seen that of the four alternatives considered it would be cheapest to order the quantity needed in two lots of 500 cartons. The EOQ is therefore 500 cartons, at which size of order the business is obtaining the best balance between the opportunity cost and the other costs. It could have been the case, if quantity discounts were larger or 'order costs' lower, that some other EOQ would have emerged.

It is now necessary to look at consumption rate in order to determine when the orders should be placed. Too soon would result in the higher stocks we are trying to avoid; too late could result in a disastrous 'stock-out' situation.

Let us suppose that the business consumes 100 cartons of supplies each week and that the EOQ is 300 cartons. Ideally, ordering would work out so that just as the last carton is used up the next delivery arrives – as shown in Fig. 13-1.

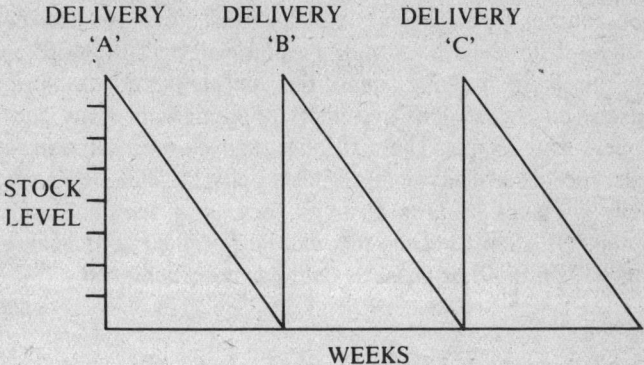

Fig. 13-1. The ideal delivery/stock level situation

This would ensure that at the same time as the business enjoys the financial benefits of an EOQ it would never have too much in stock or have it for too long. With a 100-carton consumption the first load would be ordered for delivery at the beginning of week 1, and this would last to the end of week 3, to be followed by another delivery, and so on.

Two other factors must still be taken into account to get the system right. The first is the 'lead time' that the supplier needs from receiving the order to delivery, and the second a safety margin to cover delays, strikes or other contingencies. In practice, therefore, orders must be placed at the appropriate time ahead of delivery, and timed so that consumption does not reduce stocks right down to zero. Depending on experience of suppliers' reliability, a safety margin should be built in.

SHIFTING THE COST TO THE SUPPLIER

Sometimes arrangements can be made to place a large forward order with a supplier which will be 'called-off' as required in varying quantities or delivered on pre-arranged dates. This system is popular with many suppliers as it enables them to plan their own production in advance and, if invoicing follows delivery, cuts down the buyer's stock-holding costs as these stay with the suppliers. If quantity discounts can be obtained at the same time then the best possible deal has been achieved.

GOODS IN PROCESS

Since goods in process also represent money which can neither be used nor invested, they too should be kept to a practical minimum. This is a function of production planning and, in the context of distribution, goods in process should be considered as a supply source for finished products which must be placed with the customer. The quantity of goods in process, and the speed with which they can be converted into finished product, must be taken into account when deciding the right level of finished product to hold.

FINISHED PRODUCTS

Probably the most important consideration in determining stock levels of finished product is the level of customer service required. However, once again it is important to be realistic. There will always be a temptation to hold maximum possible stocks of every product sold in order to meet every order with a prompt delivery. If this can be economically achieved then all is well, but it should be realized that the costs of providing a 100 per cent service are much greater than providing, say, a 95 per cent service. This is particularly so when several products are offered, since it will be necessary to hold sufficient stocks of all of them to meet any orders which may come along.

The effect on costs of raising service levels is shown in Fig. 13-2.

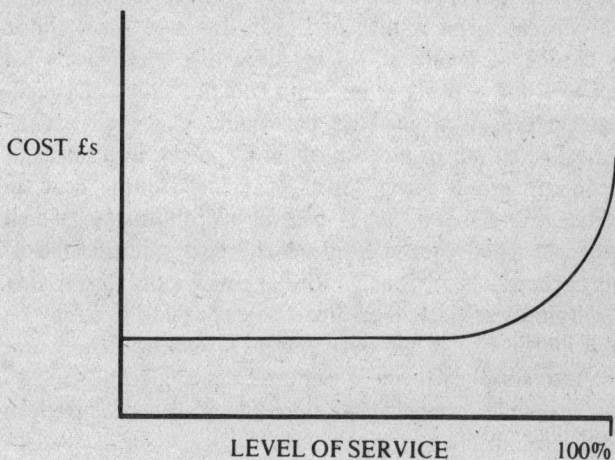

Fig. 13-2. Costs and level of service

It will be seen that the costs of meeting 95 per cent of orders immediately from stock are substantially greater than if 90 per cent are met. It is necessary to balance the service needs of the business with the cost of stock holding and the speed with which products can be provided from the production line. Ideally, all orders will be met from production with no intermediate storage, as in a jobbing production situation. There is no joy to be had from providing the world's fastest service if the business goes bust as a result.

Where to store the finished product

Yet again, in considering the location of stocks, we are looking for a balance between customer service and costs. In some cases the nature of the business severely limits the choice of location – a retailer stores his goods (at least to some extent) at his shop and the shop, or shops, must be placed where the customers can easily reach them. The owner of a chain of shops placed in a series of catchment areas spread over, say, a county, may in addition have need for a central warehouse to which wholesalers deliver and from which he supplies his shops. This approach is obviously more expensive than arranging for wholesalers to deliver direct to each shop but may be unavoidable if it is the only way in which he can ensure adequate supplies to meet demand varying from shop to shop and time to time. It all depends on the sales pattern and the reliability of suppliers.

The manufacturing business has a similar choice to make between centralized storage and dispersed storage. It may be possible to store finished products at one warehouse on or near the factory site and to make all deliveries from this central point. Alternatively, the cost of transport to customers and the service level to be provided may make a number of local warehouses necessary.

Transport costs to a local warehouse are likely to be lower than those incurred in carrying goods separately to a number of customers in the same area, as more can be carried per mile covered. There will of course be the cost of local delivery from a local warehouse to the customers

CHAPTER 14

Overhead Costs

An overhead cost is an expense incurred which cannot be directly identified with any particular item produced or service provided. The very fact that overheads cannot be directly linked to any particular production makes them a permanent threat to the unwary businessman. They tend to mount up in an insidious way until, having become a serious burden, they are suddenly noticed. In extreme cases they may be noticed so late in the day that serious damage has been done to the business.

Simon, having worked for some years for a blue-chip company, decided to start his own business making and supplying high-quality timber products such as tailor-made shelf units, small cabinets, occasional tables and the like. He aimed at the upper end of the market, selling his products direct to wealthy individuals whom he contacted by announcement in the more rarefied art magazines and 'county'-type journals.

Advertising costs mounted up and, in addition, Simon began to hold exhibitions of his work. These exhibitions – organized along the lines of an art exhibition – were held in a smart and expensive hotel which charged top rates for accommodation and also for the cocktails which Simon handed out to his invited clients.

Stationery costs were also high as Simon felt it necessary to use professionally designed letterheads, envelopes, invitation cards, etc., which were printed to a very high quality.

Simon had rented an office (in addition to his workshop) and equipped it with leased but expensive furniture, an answering machine, a photocopier, an electronic typewriter and, last but not least, sundry potted plants from a fashionable supplier.

A secretary was employed (or rather under-employed) and, when added to the charges made by his accountant, his solicitor and his bank, the cost of all this overhead was mounting up. Simon, who had not paid much attention to cash-flow forecasting or control, eventually found that his overheads amounted to about 40% of his costs. This was clearly disproportionate to his direct production costs (labour, materials, workshop and machinery) and was endangering his business.

The overheads were substantially reduced, but only after a lot of time and effort had been expended. The office was sub-let, the photocopier sold, and the potted-plant contract cancelled. The leased furniture could not be disposed of and went into storage until the leasing period expired. The secretary was persuaded to leave with a cheque for three months' pay, and Simon endured a painful but useful lecture from his bank manager when negotiating a loan to tide him over.

The first essential

The first essential is to be well aware of the level of overhead costs and then to ensure that they are controlled. Additionally, every overhead expense should be critically examined. Ask yourself the following questions:

(a) What are my overhead costs?
(b) What percentage of my total expenditure goes on overheads?
(c) Are my overhead expenses growing disproportionately?
(d) Are all my overheads absolutely essential?
(e) Are there any essential items for which I am paying too much?

Let us suppose that having asked, and answered, these questions you are not too happy with the result. What should be done about it?

I would recommend a methodical and painstaking examination of every item of overhead expenditure. The time and trouble can be very worthwhile and the result could be a dramatic improvement in profits. You may have fallen into the trap of thinking that, because your main costs (normally premises and wages) form such a large part of your total expenditure, spending time on the smaller items is only tinkering with the problem and not worth the effort. This can be very far from the truth, particularly in service businesses with high labour costs.

The example which follows is taken from real life but the figures have been 'doctored' for the sake of simplicity and the name is fictitious:

Rainbow Arts & Design Ltd rented studio premises in a suburb of London from which they provided a service to advertisers, public-relations specialists, and others requiring artwork of various kinds.

From every £100 of gross revenue received they paid out £85 in rent, rates and salaries. This expenditure was virtually irreducible and, having spent a further £10 on overheads such as postage, insurances, water rates, telephone bills, etc., they were left with an unsatisfactorily small gross profit of £5.

Rainbow Arts had tried to reduce their salary bill and also to increase prices, but both of these measures failed – and caused additional problems. They had ignored their other overheads on the grounds that they were too small to be worth bothering with. An accountant then pointed out to them that if they could reduce these other overheads by only 10% (£1) they would increase gross profit by 20%. Better still, if they could halve their overheads they could *double* their profit. This would be equivalent to doubling output and sales without any increase in the labour force. Rainbow Arts actually cut their overheads by about 30% by taking a hard, calculated look at what they were doing.

However, not all businesses are like Rainbow Arts. Some will be enjoying better profit margins, and for the owners of such fortunate concerns the Rainbow Arts example may seem unconvincing. These better-off companies can look at the subject from a different viewpoint.

Suppose that gross profit is 10% (double that of Rainbow Arts), then for every £1,000 sales revenue, £100 gross profit will be earned. It will also follow that every £100 reduction in overheads is equivalent to a £1,000 sale – with no selling or production costs! In other words, reducing overheads is an opportunity not to be missed, and it is the nearest thing there is to money for nothing.

Where To Look for Savings

Not all businesses are alike, and not all will have the same overheads to worry about. However, the list which follows will include some targets for every business.

Rent

Rental costs are virtually impossible to reduce unless (a) the landlord is unusually accommodating or (b) part of the premises can be sub-let or shared.

Prevention is better than cure in the case of accommodation costs, and great care must be taken to avoid being tempted by offices or workshops which are too large or too smart. A fancy office in an up-market area may be essential for the company image, but it is only too easy to exaggerate the need. If the only premises available are too large for estimated requirements over the first few years, it is worth checking that the terms of the lease permit sub-letting. If this is the case, it may be possible to find a sub-tenant looking for a short lease – and it may be possible to make a profit from the letting.

Otherwise, with existing premises, check out the possibilities for sharing or sub-letting. Check whether, with a lease coming to an end, it is possible to economize in the use of space and to renew the lease for part of the premises only.

One company did this simply by clearing out masses of unwanted records, dispensing with a storage area (largely filled with junk), and removing all unwanted items of furniture and equipment. On renewal of the lease they took only two of their previous three small floors in the building and saved a substantial amount – particularly because, as usual, the rent went up with the new lease.

Rates

Like rent, this is a cost which it is very difficult to do anything about. A reduction will automatically follow if total square footage is reduced as part of a rent-reduction scheme. Otherwise, nothing is lost by an appeal to the rating authority. The local inspector may be helpful.

Heat and Light

The emphasis here should be on providing a comfortable and safe level of warmth and light in the most economical way. Notwithstanding any capital costs (which might well be recouped over a period), consideration should be given to:

(a) Insulation and draught proofing. This normally yields a good return in cost saving.
(b) Replacement of electric bar heaters or fan heaters with a thermostatically controlled central system.

(c) Improving the performance of an existing central-heating system with a modern microchip-based control unit. A London company installed one for £1,400 and saved about £1,800 in oil during the next six months.

(d) Reducing the temperature of water supplied to wash basins. Such water is often too hot and a few degrees' reduction in temperature can save a good deal.

(e) Installing up-to-date strip lighting which will give a better (more even) light than the old-style bulbs at less cost in electricity. It is also worth examining whether, with existing strip lights, the most effective and economical tubes are being used. Nothing will be lost, and something may be gained, by asking a lighting manufacturer to have a look at your premises and suggest improvements. Make sure they give you an estimate of the savings to be made by any changes.

Finally, check with the electricity board that your premises are on the most economical tariff. The tariff was probably set when you started business and has not been changed despite increases in consumption.

Bank charges

Bank managers are allowed a degree of discretion in the charges made on business accounts. It is well worth shopping around, not only between one bank and another but even between branches of the same bank.

The magazine *What to buy for business*, reporting results of enquiries with banks as to charges likely to be made to a hypothetical company with a turnover of £1.5 million and a credit balance of £10,000, revealed some interesting facts. Apparently one bank estimated £356, another £1,880, while the rest quoted figures of around £1,000. The difference between the best and the worst (approximately £1,500) can represent quite a lot of sales and hard work.

A company which has no wish to change banks will not be wasting their time in protesting about the charges made. The manager probably has the authority to reduce the charges and, for the sake of a little persuasion, may agree to do so. By the way, if you feel that you have been badly treated by a bank and are in dispute with them, help might be obtainable from The Office of the Banking Ombudsman, Citadel House, Fetter Lane, London, EC4A 1BR.

Insurance premiums

Don't be afraid to argue with your insurance broker if he tells you that you cannot be properly insured at lower costs. The chances are that you can. Bear in mind that your broker, although theoretically working for you, will be tempted to place your insurance where he gets the biggest commission, and this is often the place where the price is highest. Don't hesitate to try a second broker, and in any case insist on seeing two or more quotations. Provided the policy is wide enough to cover your risks fully (including excesses and limits), and offered by a reputable insurer, you should go for the cheapest quote.

It is also worth looking seriously at your insurances to see if the business is over-insured. There is frequent comment in the business pages of the newspapers about the dangers of being under-insured, which is often the case with private insurance for houses, contents, personal effects and so on. Very little appears in the press about over-insurance.

A small firm of ship-brokers had professional liability cover of £10 million, which cost them a small fortune in premiums. In the light of the fact that the Baltic Exchange insisted on only £100,000 liability cover for its members, the ship-brokers were encouraged to reconsider their insurance. They worked out the worst imaginable scenario (i.e. the most expensive mistake they could think of) and calculated that a cover of £2 million would be quite enough. The resulting saving amounted to about 40% of their insurance costs.

General supplies

Expenditure on such items as cleaning materials, plastic refuse sacks, soap, toilet paper, and all forms of office supplies tends to mount up slowly but steadily. The cost of each individual purchase is normally only a small part of the budget and tends to go unnoticed or ignored.

Working out how much items cost in total and what they represent in terms of sales volume can be quite a shock and hence well worth the trouble. A company which did this (and was suitably horrified at the result) made representations to suppliers for discounts. About half the suppliers agreed to a reduction without any arguments. In the cases where the suppliers would not agree to a lower price, alternative quotes were obtained from other suppliers. The result was a lower price for every one of the items tackled.

Services

Apart from public services which are discussed later, most businesses employ private contractors to satisfy various needs. These include:

Laundry
Roller-towel supplies
Cleaning
Security
Delivery services
Typewriter maintenance
Computing
Payroll, etc.

In all these cases a representation to the suppliers and/or alternative quotations from competitors can result in savings.

In some cases savings can be made by the use of a little imagination and the goodwill of employees. Fred was employed by a small company which had a laundry bill too large for comfort. Hearing that arguments were going on with the laundry company, Fred approached the boss and suggested that his wife be offered the laundry contract. The result was cheaper laundry and an employee with additional reason to support and be loyal to his company. Fred's wife also turned out better work.

Check whether such services can be supplied 'in-house'. There may be unemployed or underemployed members of employees' families able and willing to type, clean offices or workshops, carry out maintenance work, and even write programmes for a computer.

Water rates

Your water rates are likely to be linked to other local rates and costs may have no relation to the amount of water used. Your local water board may allow a charging system based on a metered supply and, if your consumption is small, the result could be a significant saving. A London-based company with offices of about 30,000 square feet were paying £2,000 per month in water rates. Resulting from negotiations with the water board and introduction of a meter, their costs were reduced to £380 per month. Admittedly, this was a fair-sized office and the reduction in cost was perhaps unusually dramatic, but the story illustrates the possibilities.

Photocopying

Modern photocopiers fall broadly into two categories, viz. high-speed machines and low-speed machines. Both types may have 'additional' features such as collating or double-sided copying, and all are sufficiently expensive to warrant special consideration.

The costs of buying, leasing and maintaining the machines will be higher for those with greater speed and those with sophisticated extra features. It is important, therefore, to choose machines suited to the work required to be done, and not to be influenced by enthusiastic young salesmen into taking a machine which is unnecessarily sophisticated.

In most offices the bulk of photocopying is done in the range of 1 or 2 copies per original, although the occasional long run of, say, 100 copies can cause managers to assume that the most frequently occurring run is much more than 1 or 2. It is interesting to note that, if there is a real need for frequent long runs, a photocopier is not necessarily the cheapest way to produce them. A small offset litho machine, working from originals typed on a paper plate, is a cheap and efficient way of producing price lists, circulars, forms, instruction sheets, etc. Using an offset machine can also save printers' bills and give you control over *when* you receive your finished work. Some printers are cheap, reliable and prompt. Others are not, and having your own in-house machine can be a useful contribution to efficiency and profit.

However, if you intend to stick with a photocopier, do consider very carefully the total number of copies you will take each month. In the past the supplier's bill was usually made up for a rental charge and a copy charge. The number of copies was recorded on a meter and the bill prepared accordingly. This method has been dropped in recent years and most suppliers now apply a 'maintenance charge'. This charge is also linked to a meter which records the number of copies taken. Varying arrangements cover the 'maintenance charge', which normally starts to increase after a certain number of copies have been taken. The number of copies which triggers off the higher charge varies from one type of machine to another, and it is vital to know what situation you are faced with.

If you are taking a small number of copies from a high-speed machine your cost per copy may be enormous. The following figures illustrate the point:

Monthly rent	Minimum maintenance charge	Total	No. of copies	Cost per copy
£10	£50	£60	50	£2.40
£10	£50	£60	250	48p.
£10	£50	£60	500	24p.
£10	£50	£60	1000	12p.
£10	£50	£60	2000	6p.

The cost per copy, using the figures quoted above, only starts to reach a reasonable level when 2000 or more copies are taken per month.

A similar analysis should be made before taking on a

photocopier to ensure that the best deal is being obtained. Existing copier contracts should also be re-examined to see if savings can be made by giving notice and changing machines. Some of the options to consider are:

(a) Asking your supplier to change your machine to another in his range which suits you better.

(b) Changing to another supplier who can provide a more suitable machine.

(c) Buying a small machine outright if your copy volume is modest. Watch the maintenance costs.

(d) Using an outside print-shop for the occasional long run and the local library for the odd single copy.

Whatever you do should be carefully costed and worked out on the basis of *cost per copy*. This cost can then be compared with sending the office boy to the local library when copies are needed.

Office procedures

The savings to be achieved by looking at office procedures will probably be directly proportional to the amount of office work done. Businesses whose costs are largely made up of office expenditure stand to save most in cash terms but, as a rule of thumb, if office procedures in any business have not been reviewed in the last 12 months, a 10 per cent saving should be achievable at least.

The way to tackle the problem is to adopt the Organization and Methods (O & M) approach, asking and answering a series of questions. Each and every aspect of the work done should be subject to these questions, which are:

What is done?	Why?
How is it done?	Why?
Who does it?	Why?

Where is it done?   Why?
When is it done?   Why?

The 'why' question is the most important item and should be regarded as the acid test.

For example, suppose that a record is kept of all invoices over £50 in value. The answer to the question 'why' might be one of the following:

'Because we have always done it'
'Mr Bloggs (now retired) wanted it'
'I don't know why'
'I thought you wanted it'
'I thought it might be useful'

or even

'I didn't know we kept such a record'

Any such answer can be regarded as prima facie evidence that the record serves no useful purpose and can be scrapped. Savings will result in time, filing and paper.

Every record, routine letter, photocopy, carbon copy, file and everything else kept or done in the office should receive the same treatment, and anything which does not contribute directly or indirectly to profit should be scrapped.

Sometimes work which is useful needs simplification and the opportunity can be taken to remove unnecessary parts of an operation.

The following is a check-list of possibly fruitful lines of enquiry:

(a) Is anything done in-house which could be done more cheaply outside, e.g. payroll preparation?
(b) Are there any routine letters typed which could either be pre-printed or replaced with a compliment slip?
(c) Are there any forms which should be scrapped or re-designed?

(d) Can a small computer be *profitably* used?, e.g. for book-keeping, sales analysis, VAT records, etc. Will a computer system reduce or hold down clerical labour costs? Will a computer improve accuracy?

(e) Are there savings in time which can be gained by providing people with home-made ready reckoners or small calculators? The Post Office, for example, issues its counter clerks with a ready reckoner for working out the cost of multiple purchases of stamps. This enables the clerk *correctly* and quickly to calculate the cost of '21 stamps @ 17½p each'.

Errors present the dual penalty of the aggravation caused (e.g. an angry customer) plus the time and trouble to put things right later.

Temporary staff

Many large companies spend fortunes on temporary staff and every now and then have a great panic-stricken 'purge' to keep the cost down. Nevertheless, the expenditure goes on and on because the wrong approach is taken.

Temporaries should not be regarded as an expensive and unavoidable evil but as a way to keep down overheads. It makes good financial sense to employ temporary clerks, typists, secretaries, book-keepers or whatever in a planned way to deal with peaks of work which have been forecast. This is cheap compared with taking on a new permanent employee who will, later, be underemployed.

HOMEWORK – CHAPTER 14

14-1. By how much will you increase profit if you reduce overheads by, say, 10 per cent or 20 per cent?

14-2. How do you control overheads? Start with a thorough examination of each and every cost item.

14-3. Work your way through all the overhead costs described in this chapter. What ideas can you use? How much can you save?

14-4. Try an O & M-type exercise on your office work.

PART 4

Controlling the Finances

CHAPTER 15

Finding Out the Figures

Controlling the finances of the business, rather than allowing money (or lack of it) to control the business, requires the use of some fairly basic but essential techniques. These techniques will help you to make the right decision and avoid situations such as being forced to go cap in hand for another bank loan, finding that you cannot meet all your creditors' demands, or not having enough money to exploit a promising opportunity that comes along; in other words, to be in command.

A fatal error is to confuse the cash balance (the difference between payments and receipts) with profit. Profit is in fact very difficult to assess in any business where costs go on in the form of depreciation, expenses have to be met at some time in the future, and bad debts take some time to show themselves. Although for tax purposes, and to meet any statutory returns, a balance sheet or profit and loss account is drawn up each year, even these are only a 'snapshot' of the position at a particular time.

In chapter 4 we looked at cash-flow forecasting as part of assessing the 'money picture' of the business. To maintain control it is necessary to look ahead using such a forecast which, although inevitably imperfect, will give some prior warning of problems or opportunities so that appropriate action can be taken before it is too late.

Take the case of George and Ted:

George and Ted set up an agricultural-repair business going from farm to farm repairing tractors, combine harvesters, baling machines and the like. They had converted an old army lorry into a mobile workshop, and for the first couple of years this served them well. Costs were low and they managed quite well living from month to month and paying their bills from income as they went along.

George persuaded Ted that the business could be expanded if they had a proper workshop with a forge, a larger stock of spare parts, and various machines such as a lathe and a milling machine. Ted agreed that this would enable them to take on more work, including some of the larger jobs they could not handle with the limited resources of the mobile workshop.

In due course a workshop was found and rented (a 6-month moratorium on rent was arranged), a bank loan negotiated to buy extra equipment, and various other items including a tow truck were leased. The new, more elaborate, service was popular with local farmers who could now have major repair work done locally. Unfortunately, George and Ted did not realize that their cash-flow pattern would now change dramatically. This was due to a failure to keep income and expenditure records in the past or to estimate them for the future. The great difference was that whereas in the past they did small jobs taking, say, one or two days to complete, they were now taking on jobs requiring an elapsed time of as much as six weeks. In addition, the bills for these jobs were much larger and the 'on-the-spot' payments of the past were replaced with lengthy delays before payment was made.

Had George and Ted made a simple forecast of their cash flow for the months ahead, taking into account their fixed costs, they would have seen that they were heading for trouble. Their first 10 months, under the new scheme, turned out like this:

George & Ted's Cash Flow

	Income £	Expenditure £	Special items
January	400	280	
February	700	300	
March	700	250	
April	40	980	Stock of parts purchased
May	150	400	More parts purchased
June	150	180	
July	1000	800	Half yearly rent/rates and insurance bills
August	300	180	
September	100	200	
October	190	400	Parts purchased for autumn repair jobs

What was happening to George and Ted:

January   was a slow month with much of George and Ted's time spent in setting up the new workshop. In consequence they lost much of the winter opportunities for small repairs.

February & March   were a little better – more work was done on small jobs while George and Ted looked for large contracts. By the end of March income, so far, had exceeded expenditure by £970.

April   saw the first major job (repairing two combine harvesters) for which some major parts were purchased. George also bought a few more stock items of parts 'in case they are needed'. Income was limited because they spent almost all the month on the

	combine harvesters, and by the end of April retained income for the year so far had fallen to only £50.
May	brought £150 from small jobs and a further bill for spares resulting in a deficit for the year to date. No payment was received for the combine harvester job which, being invoiced on 1 May, was ignored by the customer until 1 June.
June	was a quiet month with farmers using much of their machinery for seasonal work, and
July, August & September	were similar. The combine harvester payment was received in July, just in time to meet the bills for rent and rates and some insurances.
October	saw George and Ted obliged to pay out yet more money on spares for the autumn repair jobs, leaving them in a parlous financial position.

Had George and Ted worked out a cash-flow forecast in advance, they would have realized that:

- January, the peak of the repair season, was the wrong time to be temporarily out of action
- Substantial sums would be needed for spare parts at a time when revenue was inadequate
- Only one major job could be done before the spring and summer seasons when machinery would be in use
- The large jobs required more time to complete and there would be long gaps between spending money and being paid

Every business needs a cash-flow forecast to warn of problems and, where cash resources are limited or income likely to be variable, such a forecast should be updated regularly and frequently.

A further advantage of cash-flow forecasting lies in the fact that it is a constant reminder of the fixed costs. George and Ted had rent and rates to pay *regardless* of how much work they did while their variable costs (mostly spare parts) were increased only when work was done.

In addition to the fixed and variable costs, allowance must also be made for a number of other elements in the income/expenditure equation, and these should be built into the cash-flow forecast:

- Maintenance – Roofs leak, machines break down, rust forms on iron tools, floors wear out, and paint will peel off the window frames
- Contingencies – A fall-back position is needed to guard against the sudden bankruptcy of a customer, a rail strike which forces the hire of an extra lorry, or a dramatic increase in interest rates which may add to out-goings
- Replacements – One day the milling machine must be replaced, the old van traded in, or a new fork-lift obtained for the warehouse

Keeping track of the fixed costs

Whether or not business is booming or slack, whether or not debtors are paying up, the fixed costs will always be with us. It is easy to overlook them in the day-to-day rush, and a useful control is to keep a fixed-cost budget, regularly checked and updated, which can be set alongside the cash-flow forecast to ensure that the fixed costs can be met on time – either from income or from resources.

Nothing very complicated is required, and a suggested format is shown below:

Item	January	February	March	April
Salaries	5000	5000	5000	5500
Rent	100	100	100	100
Rates	—	—	—	500
Insurance	350	—	—	—
Equipment lease	—	—	600	—
Van lease	120	120	120	120
Total	5570	5220	5820	6220

Making a comparison

It is also highly desirable to know how well you are doing in comparison with other ways of making a living and other companies in the same business. It is rarely possible to obtain (honestly, that is) the performance figures of a competitor, but you can ask your accountant if, in his experience, you are doing as well as you should. No respectable accountant will tell you what his other clients are achieving, but he will know whether you are doing as well.

There are other more formal sources of comparison which may be tried, including:

● Published accounts of limited companies. Such accounts must be treated with some caution as they may have been 'dressed up' for the occasion. It is worth looking at, say, three or four companies in the same line of business and taking an average of their profit/capital ratios

- Stockbrokers. Normally only available to their private clients, some stockbrokers produce reports on companies in various businesses with ratios which can be of value for comparison
- Trade associations. It is probably necessary to be a member to obtain the information
- British Institute of Management. The BIM publishes 'Interfirm Comparison' study results which are available at a modest price to non-members

Otherwise there is a standard yardstick which can be tried:
- Profit (before tax) as a percentage of capital employed. N.B. Capital should include fixed assets at present-day value, share capital, reserves, and any money borrowed from the bank or elsewhere

The result should be at least as good as the rate of return which can be obtained on a long-dated government security. If it is not, you will know that action needs to be taken – not excluding selling up and investing the proceeds in government securities!

Finally, making comparisons of your own results over the years can be revealing. The first year is almost bound to be unexciting (at least in profit terms), but a comparison between, say, years 2 and 3 using the profit/capital ratio is worthwhile. If the ratio has become less favourable in year 3, then the causes should be clearly identified and dealt with. A more favourable result in year 3 should also be closely scrutinized. It could point you in the best direction for year 4.

What do we have to do to make a profit?

Any number of businesses have failed because, despite being very active and despite much hard work, the 'break-even point' has never been calculated.

The break-even point can not only avoid the problem of flogging a dead horse, but can also be a valuable tool in setting prices, evaluating machinery, and providing a clear target to go for. The technique works using the fixed and variable costs which have already been discussed. Let us examine the technique with a very simple example:

Joe is thinking of renting a portable machine which will (on the spot) make souvenir ashtrays which he believes can be sold at seaside resorts, at exhibitions, at football matches, and anywhere else that the public can be found. The machine can be set to print an appropriate slogan on each ashtray and, if required, the name of the purchaser. Joe believes that an ashtray marked, say, 'Sam Snooks – Cup Final, Wembley 1988' will be something that Mr Snooks will want to buy.

Joe has checked on the cost involved and has drawn up a table to show what the total cost will be for various levels of sales. Joe has added to the table further columns showing prices and income. He believes that he can sell his ashtrays for £1 each, materials (variable cost) work out at 30p per ashtray, and renting the machine costs £40 per day. This is what his table shows:

Sales	£ Fixed cost	£ Variable cost	£ Total cost	£ Revenue	£ Loss	£ Profit
10	40	3	43	10	33	
50	40	15	55	50	5	
100	40	30	70	100		30
150	40	45	85	150		65
200	40	60	100	200		100
250	40	75	115	250		135
300	40	90	130	300		170

By examining this table Joe can see that if he makes and sells only 10 ashtrays he will be out of pocket by £33. If he sells 50 ashtrays, the fixed costs are spread over more sales and his loss falls to £5. He can also see that if he sells 100 ashtrays he will make a modest profit. His break-even point lies between 50 and 100 ashtrays (in fact 59).

Joe, with the help of the table, can objectively consider the position by answering the following questions:

- What is a worthwhile profit to compensate me for my efforts?
- Can I sell enough ashtrays to achieve this profit?
- How much will I be out of pocket if I have a bad day? Can I at least break even?
- How much will I make if I have a really good day and sell, say, 1000 ashtrays?
- If there is no competition and I can raise the price to £1.50, what then is my break-even price?
- If competition is fierce or sales slow, what will be the break-even point if I reduce my price to 80p?

In answering these questions (and perhaps others) Joe is establishing whether or not the venture is likely to be very risky or slightly risky. He is giving himself a 'feel' for the business and, if he goes ahead, will be able to judge from his results whether or not it is worth continuing.

It might be argued that if he sells only, say, 30 ashtrays at his first attempt, he will know it is not worth continuing without bothering with a table of figures. This is by no means necessarily the case because, with the break-even point available to him, he can assess, under the circumstances, his chances of being profitable next time. The circumstances could have included:

- Bad weather which kept the crowds away
- He started late and missed the people arriving
- He was in the wrong place, etc.

In other words, instead of giving up a potentially good opportunity, he might conclude, quite correctly, that given the right circumstances he could easily sell enough to pass the break-even point.

Increasing the turnover – a warning

As will be seen from Joe's calculations, increasing the turnover increases the profit *providing fixed costs stay the same*.

Sadly, fixed costs tend to go up and, when they do, they do so in large leaps. When planning an increase it is important to re-cost the fixed-cost budget and re-calculate the break-even point. Any increase in fixed costs will shift the break-even point further away, and the business could end up doing more business but making less profit.

Activity should therefore be increased to the maximum possible before taking on more premises, labour, machinery or whatever, and it must be realized that after taking on the additional costs a new, higher level of sales is needed to reach the new break-even point and even more to reach the former level of profit.

The best/worst case

Allied to using cash-flow forecasts, budgets and break-even calculations is another technique which can be a valuable guide and further enhance control of the finances. This technique involves preparing two or more 'scenarios' in which an attempt is made to establish the risk element of a project or development.

Scenario 1 could be an optimistic view of the project including, say, the highest level of sales believed to be achievable, top prices, low materials cost, and so on. Using these optimistic (but not unrealistic) figures, a cash-flow forecast and break-even analysis can be made and the result in profit terms determined.

Scenario 2 will then look at the opposite extreme – a pessimistic, but still realistic, view of likely circumstances. This scenario can include, in addition to modest sales figures, potential threats such as competitive action, higher interest rates, increased taxation, etc.

Having costed out both scenarios, the result may suggest that even in the worst circumstances a decent profit is on the cards. Alternatively, even the most optimistic view of the various factors may result in an unfavourable outcome. The chances are that the answer will lie somewhere between, and it may be worth trying a middle-of-the-road scenario 3.

The advantages of this type of exercise are twofold, viz:

- A serious analytical attempt has been made to evaluate the prospects, and this is far better than going in blind, or turning down the idea without giving it a chance.
- Some people are optimists by nature and some are pessimists.

The scenario method tends to balance the extreme viewpoints.

Summing up

Finding out the figures is the only way to have some control over profit, which depends on a combination of price, cost and volume. If costs go up then there is pressure for the sales price to go up and the sales volume normally falls. If costs go down then it may be desirable to reduce prices to increase sales but, on the other hand, more profit may be achievable by maintaining the price level and foregoing the extra sales. Whatever is done, the fixed costs will stay as they are – fixed.

Analysis, one way or another, is essential.

HOMEWORK – CHAPTER 15

15-1. How much in command of your finances are you? Jot down on paper any occasions in the last 12 months when you *unexpectedly* found yourself with a cash-flow difficulty.

15-2. Prepare a cash-flow forecast for the next 6 months – or, better, 12 months. Can you see from the forecast any difficult periods for which prior action is needed? Are there any significant periods of cash surplus which can be put to good use?

15-3. Find out what you can about the profit levels of other businesses similar to your own. How does yours compare? Are you doing better than if your capital was invested in a safe security?

15-4. Work out the break-even point for various parts of your operation – or, if more appropriate, the whole business. What conclusions can you draw? What future action is indicated?

CHAPTER 16

Speeding the Cash Flow

A consultant working for a major British company had been asked to examine the business from top to bottom. Profits were unsatisfactory and the board felt that there must be a number of contributory causes hidden away in all sorts of places. The consultant faithfully followed his brief and examined the workings of the various departments, staffing levels, marketing, the computer systems, and so on. When he came to make his anxiously awaited report, he said, 'Gentlemen, I will propose a number of improvements which can be made in various parts of the company, but these will be largely cosmetic. The only serious mistake that you are making is that you are not getting money in fast enough.' This, it had been discovered, was slowly crippling the business, and yet was only obvious to an outsider.

Every business is susceptible to the same ailment, and it is a never-ending requirement of management continuously to seek and apply the necessary remedies. Let's look at some of the possibilities.

Can cash sales be increased?

The market trader and many other retailers operate a purely cash business and there is no delay between parting with the goods and collecting the money. Most other businesses allow a degree of credit to their customers and suffer the problem of chasing them for payment.

Clearly, if any of the credit business can be replaced by cash sales then an improvement will be achieved. One way to do this is to look for means of 'vertical integration'. This is the jargon term meaning widening your operations to do what your suppliers, or customers, do.

Boots PLC have a successful 'upwards' vertical integration, having moved from retailing alone to manufacturing some of the products that they sell in the shops. This has the advantage of yielding greater profit since the 'price' they pay does not include the profit element which would otherwise be part of an outside supplier's price.

Vertical integration 'downwards' can mean retailing yourself the products that you normally sell to middlemen. An example is the farm shop from which the farmer obtains immediate cash payment for his eggs, vegetables and meat. The farmer, it must be pointed out, normally avoids one of the problems sometimes associated with downwards integration – that of upsetting other, bulk, customers with whom the company is now in competition. The farmer avoids this because his 'at the gate' shop is usually a long way from his other customers' outlets. The problem of upsetting bulk customers can be exaggerated, but if a means such as selling in a different area, or under another name, can be found, it may be sensible to utilize it.

Mail order may be another way to increase cash sales, provided it is done on a 'cash with order' basis. This method actually means having the cash before parting with the goods, thus completely reversing the situation.

It may, in addition, be possible to persuade bulk buyers to pay on receipt of the goods by means of a discount. Care must be taken, however, not to overdo it, and the discount must be carefully calculated with the investment value of money in mind.

Can invoices be sent earlier?

Sending out invoices promptly after delivery of the goods or service is within the control of the business itself and is clearly the first step to take where credit is given. There should be no delays, for example, in waiting for an invoice to be typed some time after delivery. This delay can be avoided by having a three-part set of forms, with the invoice as the top sheet and the copies constituting delivery note and receipt respectively. If required, the price can be obliterated on the delivery note and receipt by means of printers' ornaments, leaving date, description of goods and other data clearly carboned through. Using this method also avoids errors such as having a different quantity or description on the invoice which will give the customer a first-class argument for delaying payment while his query is sorted out.

Saving even a day or two in the invoicing process can have a significant effect, especially at the end of the month. Many businesses have a regular monthly computer-run to process invoices received and prepare the payments due on them. Missing this monthly run can mean having to wait a whole month or more before payment. If a complaint is made to the customer, then back will come the answer, 'I'm sorry, there is nothing I can do as it's all on the computer.'

The target should be to send out the invoice within 24 hours of receipt of delivery, or completion of the service. Any longer means that money is being wasted.

Can invoiced amounts be smaller?

A corollary of sending invoices earlier is the avoidance of putting two or more deliveries on one invoice. Not only is time lost in holding up payment for the first delivery while the second is taking place, but the size of the debt may have a bearing on the speed of payment. The reasons for this are:

- Many companies put high-value invoices through a more rigorous checking procedure which takes longer

- Payments of large amounts may require approval at a higher level by a VIP who is very busy on other matters
- Companies with a cash-flow problem may deliberately delay payment of large amounts until they have some money in from their own debtors

Chasing the unpaid bill

STAGE 1 – STATEMENTS

Many companies ignore invoices and pay on statements so, once again, it is important to send them out without delay. Every unpaid amount should appear on the statement, which in itself will act as a reminder and, with a pre-printed message, can remind customers of your payment terms.

STAGE 2 – THE TACTFUL TELEPHONE CALL

Because an amount is overdue does not necessarily mean that the customer is deliberately delaying payment. He may be genuinely waiting for the computer-run or have staff away with the 'flu or any one of a number of other difficulties. A polite and fairly gentle reminder could be enough to persuade him to put your invoice on top of the pile.

STAGE 3 – A WRITTEN REMINDER

The written reminder, sent about a month after the phone call, can be rather more formal and more firmly worded. If, after a further month, there has been no response, it will be necessary to move to stage 4.

STAGE 4 — THE FIRST WARNING

A letter should be written pointing out how long the payment is overdue and that reminders were given on such and such dates. A new deadline for payment can be set with a statement that legal action will be considered if payment is not forthcoming on or before that date.

In most cases the threat of legal action brings a response and, in cases where it does not, the chances are that the customer is unable to pay rather than unwilling to pay. Whether or not legal action is taken will depend on a number of factors, including:

● The amount of money in question. Your legal costs may be more than the debt due to you. A compromise, which costs less than court action, is a letter from your solicitor to the customer. This has no more force in law than a letter you may write yourself, but it suggests that you mean business

● There may be evidence (e.g. other people complaining of overdue payments) that the customer is penniless and possibly going, or gone, out of business. Any money spent in pursuing the debt will probably be wasted

● The public relations aspect. The appearance of your company as a plaintiff in a local court may be a means 'pour encourager les autres' or may be bad for your image and damage sales in the future

If, however, the sum of money is large, and it is believed that the customer can be made to pay, do not hesitate to go ahead with legal action. You may feel you will be losing 'a good customer', but that was something you lost when the debt became seriously overdue. Good customers who do not pay are not good customers at all.

Debt-collection agencies

There are firms specializing in debt collection who work for a percentage of the amount owed. Care should be taken in selecting such an agency, as there are some shady characters around whose methods leave something to be desired and whose actions may rebound on you. Your accountant or solicitor may be able to suggest a reputable firm.

Factoring

Many of the major banks have subsidiary companies who offer a factoring service involving:

- Keeping your sales ledger, preparing and despatching your invoices.
- Keeping track of outstanding debts and chasing them.

Factoring companies also maintain information on the credit-worthiness of business concerns, and can advise you of credit ratings if you are uncertain as to whether or not credit terms should be given to a prospective new customer.

However, the three major benefits are:

- You save money through not having to keep your own sales ledger
- The factoring company will normally guarantee payment
- Part of the value of each invoice (probably about 80 per cent) will be paid to you as soon as the invoice is despatched

In return, of course, the factoring company will require a fee, and it is up to you to weigh up the value of the service against the cost. Your bank is probably the best source of advice on where to find a good factoring company and what their terms are.

These are some of the ways and means of speeding up the receipt of money due, but it is also important to build into your business routines designed to prevent the overdue money problem in the first place.

DO YOU ASK FOR REFERENCES BEFORE GIVING CREDIT?

Granting any significant degree of credit to an unknown individual or company without checking their financial standing is a risk seldom worth taking. The larger the order, the greater is the temptation to accept it, but greater too is the risk. Obviously requests for referees must be handled tactfully, but any really professional businessman will understand and respect your reason for doing so. Any belligerent reaction to what is a perfectly normal business procedure should be treated with considerable suspicion.

CAN MONEY BE PAID 'UP-FRONT'?

Asking for a deposit, or something on account, is becoming increasingly common in these difficult times and, where goods are made to order (e.g. built-in furniture, clothing and machine tools), it is prudent to do so. Not only will this practice guard against defaulters, but it will also provide funds for raw materials and other variable costs involved in the job.

CAN CREDIT-CARD PAYMENTS BE ENCOURAGED?

Although a small percentage of the value of each transaction must be paid to the credit-card company, the seller has the benefit that payments are guaranteed. The use of credit cards applies mainly in retail-shop and mail-order businesses, but there seems to be no reason why others, such as plumbers, business consultants or interior decorators, should not do the same. It is worth thinking about.

IS THERE A SIMPLE, CHEAP BUT EFFECTIVE PROCEDURE IN OPERATION TO SEE WHEN BILLS ARE OVERDUE FOR PAYMENT?

There are all kinds of computer systems, card indexes and patent ledger systems available for recording debts and indicating when they are due. Some of these systems are expensive to install and require careful attention if they are to be operated effectively. Having to look up entries in a book, for example, can be a chore and can be forgotten.

The simplest, and easiest, way is to make your own copy invoices do the work for you by placing them, visibly, in a container marked with the payment date. One such system, operated by a small printing company, uses three 'concertina' files. Each section in the file represents, and is marked with, a working day, and into it is placed any invoice due to be paid on that day. This, without any records at all, tells the clerk in charge which invoices are due for payment each day and, by comparison with today's date, any which are overdue and by how long. The 'first' file covers the present month, and the others the next two months. As one becomes cleared it is used to start another record for the third month ahead.

Variations on this idea may be preferred, such as using boxes with compartments marked by week or month, or by having a special 'overdue folder' into which outstanding invoices are placed when payments are outstanding for more than, say, seven days. The 'overdue folders' might be kept on the manager's desk for his personal attention and to enable him to see, at a glance, if there is any significant indebtedness.

The other side of the coin – paying for supplies

This aspect of the business is one where, within limits, efforts should be made to avoid the message in the title of this chapter – 'Speeding the cash flow'. When paying out, the usual preference is to slow down the cash flow. The objective should be to seek legitimate and fair ways to do it without damaging your reputation and business. Suppliers who are treated badly may well discontinue giving credit and, possibly, spread the word that your business is giving them trouble.

Where a business has had a good relationship with a supplier, and payments have been made on time, it may well be possible to negotiate a longer period of credit in temporary periods of difficulty. Most suppliers will want to keep and encourage a hitherto valued customer, and will often meet an honest and open request for easier terms. It is essential, however, that these terms, if granted, are adhered to.

Suppliers may, in any case, be prepared to grant better terms either in payment periods or discounts to a respected and long-standing customer, and it is well worth making an approach. Alternatively, it is often possible to negotiate a bulk order at reduced price coupled with an arrangement to 'call-off' the supplies at regular intervals. Such arrangements will assist suppliers in their own forward planning and may well be attractive enough to them to prompt more favourable terms.

Perhaps it is unnecessary to say that all invoices should be checked to see that they accurately represent the deliveries made, and that the business is not being charged for something it did not order or receive. It is of course quite legitimate to withhold payment while a genuine error is being cleared up.

Selling off the surplus

No opportunity should be lost in selling off any unwanted stock, machinery, office equipment or whatever. It is not unknown for businesses to have idle equipment (probably bought for a particular job or project) which is gathering dust and occupying valuable space. Whatever amount of money was paid for such items, and whatever 'book value' they may have, it is better to dispose of them and convert them into cash which can be usefully applied elsewhere in the business. Keeping unused or unwanted items amounts to a loss of income, at least to the extent that any sale value could be sitting in a building society account earning interest.

HOMEWORK – CHAPTER 16

16-1. Brainstorm ways to increase your cash sales. If one or two of the best ideas are applied, what effect will this have on profit?

16-2. How good is your invoicing system? Review the system, check how it works, and the time lag between fulfilling the order and mailing the invoice. Try to find a way to cut, say, 25 per cent from the time lag.

16-3. Try, as far as practicable, an experiment by invoicing in smaller amounts. Monitor the results to see if there is an overall improvement in payment time.

16-4. Review your 'chase-up' system for outstanding debts. How effective is it? Should you be tougher?

How do you know which payments are overdue – is the system effective?

16-5. Consider the potential benefits of using a debt-collection agency or a factoring company. Find out how they work. Find out the experiences of others who use them. Would such services suit your business?

16-6. Work out some ideas for obtaining better credit terms from suppliers. Can this be done without loss of discounts, or will other benefits exceed the value of the discounts?

CHAPTER 17

Minimizing Tax

Avoiding tax (as opposed to evading tax) is a matter of organizing yourself and the business to take maximum advantage of the tax laws and rules. The job of organizing to obtain maximum advantage is made more difficult because of the readiness with which successive governments and Chancellors of the Exchequer will change the rules. This means that regular re-appraisals must be made to get the best out of changing circumstances, and also that skilled professional advice needs to be obtained to ensure that the 'small print' details and complexities are properly understood and allowed for. A review of the situation should be made at least annually, and probably after the latest budget – the occasion when the Chancellor is more likely to move the goal-posts.

Carrying out such a review requires, in some businessmen, a change of attitude. What, you may ask, has attitude to do with it? In fact, quite a lot, as the wrong attitude can bring about a weak spot in the management of our business affairs.

Most of us have moments when we feel, understandably, that taxes and the tax system are nothing more than diabolical obstacles to our progress, dreamed up by a stupid and malevolent government. We regard the annual tussle with the tax inspector with as much enthusiasm as we have for a bout of toothache and, as with toothache, we tend to put the subject out of our minds as much as possible.

This attitude can lead to neglect of a vital point, which is that tax is *another business expense* and should be treated as such. Time will be taken to control other expenses such as wages, fuel bills, telephone charges and so on, so why not tax expenses too?

To be able to carry out any effective control on tax expenses requires at least a working knowledge of the tax system and, although competent professional help is necessary to cope with the complexities, the businessman should not abdicate wholly in favour of a professional. There are a number of ways in which the informed businessman can take advantage of the tax system and can avoid unnecessary tax obligations, and he should equip himself with the basic knowledge necessary to do so.

Fortunately, dealing with tax is not wholly a matter of coping with more and more onerous impositions on business. Governments do, from time to time, make life easier for businesses by, for instance, changes to allowances designed to encourage business of one kind or another. Any potential advantage must be exploited to the maximum possible extent, and this can best be done if the business is organized in the best possible way to respond to changes and the owner of the business knows how to do it.

Gaining the necessary knowledge

A good starting-point for learning about tax are the booklets published by the Inland Revenue. These give the official position and, although sometimes slightly heavy going, the authorities have, it seems, done their best to make them understandable to the layman. Some of the booklets have been in existence for some time, so it is important to obtain the latest version plus any supplements that have been printed. The supplements update the original booklets.

The following is a selection of the booklets available:

IR 9	Notes on treatment of livestock kept by farmers and other traders
IR 11	Tax treatment of interest paid
IR 14 & 15	Construction Industry Tax Deduction Scheme
IR 16	Share acquisitions by directors and employees
IR 18	Corporation tax
IR 26	Changes of accounting date
IR 28	Starting in business
IR 35	Income tax: profit sharing
IR 51	The Business Expansion Scheme
CA 1	Capital allowances on machinery or plant
CA 2	Capital allowances on industrial buildings
CGT 1	Capital Gains Tax: how to calculate your gains
CGT 8	Capital Gains Tax
CGT 11	Capital Gains Tax and the small businessman

Having read the booklets appropriate to your business, it will be useful to read a general book on the subject of tax. Such books can be found in public libraries, and there is often a wide choice of easy-to-read volumes written with the layman in mind. It is not necessary to read a *textbook* on tax – these are normally very specialized and written for people making a living from taxation work, such as solicitors, accountants and certain bank employees.

Having completed your reading, you should be in a position to ask yourself various questions on your taxes and your business, e.g.:

• Is my business the best type of trading entity for tax purposes?

- How will my plans for the future be affected by taxation?
- Is there anything that I, or my tax adviser, have overlooked and which needs acting upon?

Let us now take a brief look at two of the areas about which you will have gained some knowledge and about which you may have some queries in mind.

What type of business is best?

Most new businesses start up as 'sole proprietor' concerns, or are formal or informal partnerships of two or three people. This type of business offers clear tax advantages in the early stages as a result of tax being assessed on a previous-year basis. This means that there will be a considerable delay in paying tax after the start-up, thus leaving money in the business to be used for development. However, as the years pass and the business grows, it may become desirable to form a limited company. Profit will, hopefully, increase steadily after the early stages, and it must be remembered that individuals or partners must pay tax on these profits whether they are drawn or not. A limited company pays corporation tax and, although this tax will be assessed on an 'actual basis' and is payable nine months after the accounting period, the rate may well be lower.

What business expenses can be claimed?

It is easy, with no methodical way of doing it, to overlook an item of expense which can be claimed against tax. The tax inspector is unlikely to be so helpful as to suggest that something has been forgotten; the onus rests upon the owners of the business to ensure that every possible allowance is claimed. The following is a broad check-list of the likely items which can be claimed, which should be reviewed and updated if and when changes to the tax rules are made:

- Wages and salaries paid to employees – full- or part-time. The sole proprietor should not forget any payment made to his or her spouse, but care should be taken to see that this payment is genuine and actually made. Any such payment will be tax-free up to the level of personal allowance
- Raw materials and other supplies
- Minor capital items such as calculating machines, small tools and typewriters. (Major capital items such as vehicles are dealt with differently under the tax rules – normally on a 'writing down' basis reflecting depreciation.)
- Leasing costs and hiring charges
- Insurances and other overheads such as heating, lighting, telephone.
- Delivery costs
- Travel costs (with certain limitations)
- Legal and other professional fees – but *not* for 'non-trading' matters such as advice in respect of a property lease
- Interest on loans. Such loans must be incurred solely for, and in relation to, the business
- Bad debts. The tax inspector may well demand proof that there is no prospect of being paid the money due to you
- Outstanding creditors. These may be items of expense which the business has incurred but not yet paid. These may be allowable as a cost in the tax period being assessed
- Subscriptions to trade associations or professional bodies

- Entertaining of foreign customers. Any such claim will be likely to prompt the inspector to demand evidence of your level of export business
- Small gifts. The value of gifts allowable may change from time to time but has always been at a miserly level!
- Services – e.g. cleaning, laundry and security

These are some of the items of business expense for which claims may be allowed. The records of the business should be geared to provide the figures easily and in full – backed up by evidence in the form of wages records and receipts.

You may by now have decided that your tax adviser may not have given you as good a service as you would wish or, if you have managed so far without a tax adviser, that you should employ one quickly! There are two subjects to be considered; namely, choosing your tax adviser, and how best to work with him.

Choosing your tax adviser

Although most of us think of accountants as tax advisers, in fact they come in several forms. Accountants do not have a monopoly of tax knowledge; indeed, some of them are not tax experts at all. Members of the Institute of Taxation, solicitors, and even retired tax inspectors can offer a good alternative. The essential attributes to look for are:

- A good knowledge of your type of business and experience of dealing with the tax problems peculiar to your type of business
- Adequate time to give you a good, prompt service.
- Willingness at least, and enthusiasm if possible, for dealing with businesses of your size

- A basic qualification (e.g. by examination)

However, these attributes alone should not be the only criteria on which your choice should be based. You will have to work *with* your tax adviser, pay his bills and, to some extent, depend on him. Clearly the more knowledge you have gained yourself, the less dependent you will be, but you should be satisfied also on the following points:

- The person concerned is someone with whom you feel you can develop a rapport – in short, you will get on well together
- That you are not being regarded by him as someone highly privileged to be his client. Some professionals, in a number of fields, adopt this lofty attitude which serves as a barrier to constructive discussion to the detriment of the client

When talking to him, do not be bashful. Find out from him not only what he expects to charge for his services (a quotation for the first year) but also how he will charge.

Ask him to give you an off-the-cuff opinion of how your present tax liabilities can be reduced or delayed. This will give you an idea as to how knowledgeable and imaginative he is, but of course you must give him some information to go on – perhaps the previous year's figures. You might also ask him for a timetable of the work he could do for you, including a review of your tax position and completion of your next tax return.

If you do not understand what he is saying, assuming you have gained a working knowledge of the subject as suggested above, then you may be talking to the wrong person. At all events, do not give up until you *do* understand because, if he is to be your tax adviser in the future, it is essential that you can communicate with him and he with you.

Even if you are sufficiently satisfied with the results of these 'tests' to give him your work, the testing period has not come to an end. The acid test is the result of his efforts, and to obtain the best result some responsibility rests on you. The manner in which you work with him will affect, for good or ill, the level of success achieved.

Working with your tax adviser

The best results will be achieved by working closely together. This includes keeping your adviser fully informed about your activities and, in particular, your future plans. Any plan for development or change to your business should be discussed with your tax adviser *before* any action is taken. It is frustrating at best to be told, after you are committed, 'What a pity you did that, Mr Bloggs; if I had known I could have told you that taking a partner at this time will cost both of you some tax which could have been avoided.'

Avoid also the temptation under the day-to-day pressures gradually to leave things more and more in your adviser's hands without checking with him what he is doing. Some tax advisers, like some lawyers, will pursue a small point to the bitter end with copious correspondence with the tax inspector, research into legal precedents, and even consultation with other tax experts. This may be all very well, but you are paying for it and any resulting savings may be less than the cost of achieving them. If there is a point to be made with the inspector, it is sometimes better to ignore any past happenings and to aim to get things right in the next financial year. Make sure also that your adviser tells you of any query that he receives from the tax inspector regarding your accounts, and that you understand what is going on. Anything agreed between the inspector and the adviser is likely to have long-term effects, and you should be in a position to approve (or disapprove) in advance.

All of this adds up to you being in command of the situation, using the knowledge you have gained.

On the other hand, you must be absolutely fair to your tax adviser by giving him all the information he needs or is likely to need and, above all, being scrupulously honest with him. Tell him what you are doing and what your objectives are, but don't be too dogmatic. Allow him room to *advise* you, rather than just complete your tax return, and once you are satisfied that he knows his stuff, show respect for his professional skills by letting him use them.

Working *together* is the best method of finding ways to minimize your taxes.

Having achieved a good and effective relationship with your tax adviser you can, once again using your own acquired knowledge of the tax scene, plan your future in a more effective way.

Future developments and tax

In addition to the taxation involved in your regular business operations, there will be tax implications in every change you make. Should you decide to expand the business by acquisition, buy or rent an additional building, stockpile a raw material or whatever, the tax angle must be checked. In other words, your future plans must be checked out in terms of tax and any appropriate adjustments made.

Among the possible changes that you might be considering are the following. These could well have tax aspects which, when rooted out, might make all the difference between a 'go' or 'no go' decision:

- Factoring your debts
- Purchase of capital items
- Leasing
- Raising finance
- Exporting
- New products

As an example, suppose you were considering increasing your discount for prompt payment as a result of a cash-flow problem. You might then compare the cost of this (i.e. the lost income) with the after-tax interest costs of a loan to tide you over.

Alternatively, you may be thinking about acquiring a small office building – an asset which will probably increase in value over the years but which is not likely to qualify for capital allowances. It may be possible to borrow the money personally from a bank or finance house and rent the building to the company. The loan interest can then be deducted from your personal rental income when calculating your personal tax bill.

Providing for retirement

It may seem odd to include planning for your retirement in a chapter dealing with minimizing taxes. In fact the two are closely linked, as there is a substantial tax incentive in providing yourself with a pension. This tax incentive has been with us for many years through successive governments and, although it was under attack in 1985, looks as though it will survive for some time yet – hopefully indefinitely.

Before considering a pension plan it is necessary to decide what you wish to do with the business when you reach the end of your working days. Some businesses, such as one-person consultancies, will have virtually no sale value on the departure of the proprietor, and for such people a pension plan is probably essential.

The owner of a business with a sale value by virtue of assets and 'goodwill' has at least two other options:

- The business can be sold and the proceeds invested to provide a retirement income, e.g. by means of an annuity
- The business can be 'kept in the family' with the original owner retaining a share and living on the dividends or a 'consultancy fee'

There are personal taxation angles to be considered carefully in respect of these options but, assuming that you decide on a pension, then the business taxation incentive can be exploited. The incentive lies in the fact that any money paid into an *approved* pension scheme is, within limits, allowed as a deductible expense. In addition, when the pension is eventually paid to you, part of it will be regarded as repayment of capital and will be free of tax.

Simply saving money to buy an annuity does not attract these tax benefits, and even if you invest the savings as you go along you will not do as well at the end of the day.

An alternative to be looked at if you own a company, as opposed to being a sole proprietor or partner, is to set up a self-administered pension fund so that the company makes pension contributions for the directors.

There are many schemes available and regularly advertised and, in addition to comparing one with another, it is strongly recommended that qualified professional advice is obtained before making a decision. A solicitor can advise on this matter, and in view of the potential tax saving, it is well worth the fee.

A word about VAT

Value Added Tax replaced purchase tax in 1973 and is now well established as another and different tax system. VAT is the responsibility of Customs and Excise, the officers of which have wide powers to investigate suspected irregularities – including powers to search premises.

Anyone considering voluntary registration for VAT or who, by virtue of turnover must or has registered, is well advised to read and carefully digest the explanatory booklets available from their local Customs and Excise office. Records and accounts must be kept in a manner satisfactory to the Customs and Excise, VAT invoices prepared according to laid-down procedures, and quarterly returns submitted on time. Penalties for failure can be severe, and I recommend a chat with your local VAT man if in any doubt as to what is required.

Voluntary registration is open to anyone in business, even if they have not reached the turnover level which makes registration obligatory. This has the advantage of giving the appearance of having a higher turnover than is actually the case and can be good for the image.

It also becomes possible to claim 'input VAT' paid on telephone bills, petrol, etc., but *not* on entertaining or company cars. The disadvantage is the obligation to charge VAT on your own invoices, thus increasing your price but, of course, with no financial gain to yourself. You also have the burden of the records and returns.

HOMEWORK – CHAPTER 17

17-1. Do you feel 'comfortable' on tax matters? Can you discuss tax confidently with your tax adviser, or do you largely ignore the subject as being one for the specialist only? Unless you feel well on top of the subject, learn the basics using the material suggested in this chapter.

17-2. Review your tax position, with or without your tax adviser. Are you claiming all the permitted allowances?

17-3. Is your business the right type from a tax point of view? For instance, should you form a limited company?

17-4. Are you satisfied with your tax adviser? How much has he saved you? If appropriate, seriously consider a change.

17-5. Practise working constructively with your tax adviser. Do you give him all the information he needs to do a good job for you? Do you discuss changes to your business with him – before taking action?

17-6. What are your plans for retirement? Are you taking advantage of pension-plan tax concessions?

PART 5
How to Make it Happen

CHAPTER 18

What Do You Want?

By the time you have reached this chapter a number of things should have been done. Some of the opportunities and problems facing the business should have been identified and evaluated, the market and sales analyzed, and the finances examined in a variety of ways. Hopefully, ways and means have been worked out to reduce costs and increase income and generally to make the best possible use of the resources available. Some of the ideas developed may have been implemented and the benefits seen.

It is to be hoped that the profit-making capacity of the business has been developed to its maximum and, if so, decisions must be taken on the question of where to go from here. A range of options will be available, but let us first examine your wishes as the owner of the business.

What are your ambitions and needs?

Some people are never content, no matter how much material wealth they accumulate, while others can achieve satisfaction and happiness with a modest degree of comfort and possessions. Some people yearn for villas on the French Riviera, a yacht anchored at Antibes, and a new Rolls Royce or Mercedes every year. Whatever it is that the owners of a business seek and strive for they should be able, by this stage, to know whether the business as it stands can give it to them.

The lucky man who finds complete satisfaction with what the business provides now can afford to relax just a little and draw up a plan to stay roughly where he is. The more ambitious must view the business as it is now as merely a stage in a process of growth and development – perhaps with no positive or defined final result.

You may have started with clear ideas of where you wanted or hoped to go, but it is possible that, influenced by the experience involved in reaching the present situation, you have reviewed your ideas either upwards or downwards. Whatever the case, now is the time to do some self-questioning. Further expansion is unlikely to be any less demanding of time, worry and sweat, and there is also some truth in the saying 'the bigger they are the harder they fall'. On the other hand, the business may be more secure if it grows and/or diversifies. Some of these expansion possibilities will be examined in the next chapter, but at this point it is important to clarify your ambitions and wants. This can be done by answering a series of questions:

- Am I satisfied with the profits I currently enjoy?
- How much more profit do I need to satisfy my wants?
- Must I, in any case, expand the business to make it more secure? e.g. because the business is too dependent on one or two major customers
- If expansion is preferred or necessary, am I willing to take on even more work and worry, or can I see a clear way to delegate some of this to branch managers or other staff?
- Regardless of the financial rewards, security of the business, the work load, etc., do I enjoy myself so much that I want to develop further for that reason?

These are sample questions and there may be others, more appropriate to you as an individual or your particular business. Their relevance, and the justification for spending time on them, relates to the need consciously and objectively to decide what you want. It is only too easy to work on from day to day and week to week being carried by circumstances into new levels of activity, or different activities, without standing back and saying, 'Hold on a minute, do I really want this?' The whole purpose of running your own business is to give you what *you* want, and it is on the basis of these wants that the future should be planned.

Assuming that you know what you want, it is now possible to examine some of the options open to you. Remember that I am also assuming that you have accomplished the objectives mentioned in the first paragraph of this chapter, namely the best use of resources as the business stands now.

Some of the options

Dependent on the results of the self-questioning, you may opt for:

- Closing down and perhaps starting again in a new line of business
- Keeping things more or less as they are
- Going for more expansion by increasing market share and output of your present products or service
- Expanding by going into different markets, creating different products, or a combination of both
- Expanding to a pre-determined target size, market share or income level or some combination of these

Examination of these options should lead you to decide on a target or objective for the future and, to achieve it, a plan. You are now getting into 'Corporate Planning' or 'Long-Range Planning', beloved (for good reason) of big businesses. Such planning is almost essential for success (almost, because, although unlikely, it is possible to get there by sheer luck) and is worth taking time and trouble over.

The basic concept is illustrated in Fig. 18-1.

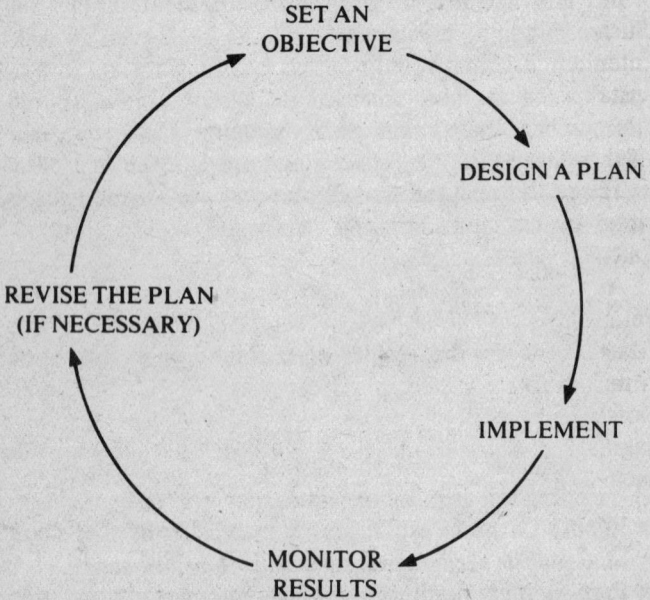

SET AN
OBJECTIVE

DESIGN A PLAN

REVISE THE PLAN
(IF NECESSARY)

IMPLEMENT

MONITOR
RESULTS

Fig. 18-1. The planning-cycle

Developing the plan

The first step in developing the business plan is to define the objective in as precise a way as possible. This precision is necessary in order to plan in a practical and realistic way and to avoid any woolly ideas which are likely to remain as pipe-dreams. Do not, for example, state your objectives as:

'To expand as much as possible'

or 'To make more profit'

or 'To take a larger share of the market'

Such objectives are almost meaningless, even if well intentioned, and give you nothing positive to go on. For instance, what does 'as much as possible' mean? Also, *how much* more profit? Again, how much larger a share of the market?

The objectives should set some target against which progress is measurable and from which it is possible to calculate what has to be done.

An objective such as, 'To expand the business on the retail side to obtain 50 per cent of the sales in the Manchester area by 1988 while maintaining gross profit at a minimum of 8 per cent of capital employed' makes it possible to work out a plan to achieve the objective taking into account the things to be done. These might include:

- Finances – where will the money come from?
- Staff – what recruitment and training will be needed?
- Premises – will more space be necessary?
- Timing – what are the best times to do things? How much time will be needed to accomplish the various steps?
- Marketing – what needs to be done in the way of publicity, sales force and promotion?
- Control – how will progress be judged? What facts and figures must be recorded?

Designing such a plan and all the work it entails will improve the chances of success considerably. The proof of this lies in the experience of many businesses, when working out the programme, of finding that the objective is actually impossible to achieve. In other words, the planning puts you on the best track and can, in extreme cases, show you before time and money has been wasted that you are heading the wrong way. In such cases the objective needs to be reviewed and the process started again.

This type of experience also underlines the fact that answering the question 'What do you want?' may well start with a simple answer such as 'To be very much richer' but of necessity must be followed up by some quite detached thinking, research and calculation. In other words, it is necessary, having decided what you want from a purely personal basis (e.g. the villa by the Med. and the luxury yacht), the ways and means of getting these must be worked out by hard, cold, business reasoning.

In the next chapter we will examine ways and means of expanding – including diversifying – which can yield particular advantages. However, before looking at the various possibilities it is a good idea to consider carefully another important ingredient of your long-range plan – how fast do you want to go?

Some people are only truly happy when they are in a frantic hurry and, as an estate agent once said, 'What I really enjoy is all the cliff-hanging and wheeler-dealing in this business.' Others prefer a more steady and predictable life, taking things in easily digestible stages with time to reflect, reconsider and revise.

Time should also be spent deciding whether you would prefer a gradual increase in your business or whether you would be motivated by taking some fairly substantial steps.

I must stress that these questions are still on the

personal level of what you as an individual would be most happy with. There will of course be restrictions on what you can in practice achieve – not least finding the necessary capital. It is, however, important to be sure what you want because, once launched in a particular direction, it may be difficult and expensive to change course.

For those who are content to stay where they are, what follows in chapter 19 should still be relevant. Ideas for improving the present business may be found and, who knows, you may well be tempted to have a go at a bigger future after all.

HOMEWORK – CHAPTER 18

18-1. *Write down* in clear unambiguous terms your ambitions for yourself and your business.

18-2. Are you progressing towards your ambition or are you being carried along by the tide of events? If the latter, prepare one or two *outline* plans to bring yourself back on target.

18-3. Examine the options described in this chapter and consider, again, your outline plans. Review the plans to suit any second thoughts.

18-4. Now develop your chosen plan using the planning-cycle – starting with a clear, unambiguous statement of your objective.

18-5. Re-read your plan several times over a period of two to three weeks and review/polish it as you do so. Discuss the plan with your employees and your professional advisers. Revise again on the basis of any ideas they have.

18-6. Are you now clear about what you want and where you are going? If you are, chapter 19 will give you some practical guidance on making it happen.

CHAPTER 19

Ways to a Bigger Future

By now you have come a long way. You have in the first
five chapters examined and analyzed your present position
and, in chapters 6–8, considered ways and means to use
existing resources more profitably. Add to this a cost-
reduction programme, better control of the finances and
a rethink of your objectives, and you are well placed to
go for growth – if that is what you want.

In this chapter we will examine the ways and means to
bring growth to the business, and in some respects we
will be looking again at some of the concepts of earlier
chapters, but in a different context. The homework
already done will be useful – in particular the homework
from chapters 6, 7 and 8. It is recommended that you
refresh your memory on this work and have it close to
hand when reading this chapter.

Looking back to the beginning

When you started your business you will have encountered various problems, possibly disappointments where
people let you down, help from various quarters, and
experiences which made you change your views on something or other. You may have had experiences which
made you say, 'That is something I will never do again',
or, 'I will remember that, it may be useful in future.'

Now is the time, when deciding the best way to make
your business grow, when all those initial experiences can
be put to good use. It is first necessary, however, to sort

out the lessons you learned and, as recommended earlier in this book, to put them down on paper.

- What problems did you encounter – how did you solve them?
- What circumstances or people helped you?
- What circumstances or people hindered you?
- What action would you avoid in future and why?
- What actions did you conclude were very necessary and why?

An analysis such as this will be useful to you now for the simple reason that you are likely to encounter the same or similar situations again – possibly on a larger scale.

You can now also put to good use all the homework you have done in the earlier chapters. Everything you have decided about your product or service, your market, your resources (staff, premises, etc.) will be relevant to the various alternative 'ways' to the future described in this chapter. To make it easier to apply this knowledge (or decisions), I have used similar headings to those you encountered before and, where appropriate, have included some 'memory-jogging' paragraphs.

The alternative ways to grow

EXPANDING THE EXISTING BUSINESS

As opposed to diversifying in some way, possibly the most obvious way to grow is to expand what you are doing now. This can include setting up branches offering the same service or product, adding to your manufacturing capacity, taking on more staff, stepping up the selling activities, or some combination of these.

Expanding what you are presently doing has these advantages:

- You are familiar with the product, market and other aspects of the business
- You will be offering a more acceptable idea to a potential financial backer than if you are trying to raise funds for a venture that you have little or no experience of
- Your employees will also have experience and familiarity with existing operations
- You may be able to achieve 'economies of scale'. For example, it may not be necessary to double your labour costs to double output and sales

Financing an expansion programme is clearly a vital ingredient, as it is if you are seeking to buy a business, enter a franchise agreement, or attempting any other method to enlarge your operation. Since the ways to deal with financing are similar in every case, and the topic is so crucial, the subject is dealt with separately in a later part of this chapter. It is necessary in any case to first complete various 'studies' in order to know how much additional funding will be necessary. These studies will form the basis from which the expansion plan will be designed.

STUDY I – THE MARKET

Your decision to expand may be 'market-led'. That is to say that demand for the product or service is so great that it cannot be satisfied from existing resources, and you know that more sales can be made if the product is available. This is an ideal situation which, if you don't move fast enough, may be exploited by a competitor coming in to fill the gap.

Alternatively, and more commonly, the businessman will have come to the conclusion that *with increased selling effort*, and/or increasing population of potential customers, more sales can be made.

Whatever the case, a cold-blooded evaluation of the market must be made (see Homework, chapter 3). If you have a new product in mind, do not make the mistake of assuming that a market will appear for it without first researching to confirm the position. For instance, you will need to estimate how much more selling effort will be needed and how much this will cost in wages, advertising, vehicle costs, etc.

STUDY 2 – PREMISES

Will your expansion require new or additional premises? To answer this question it is necessary to be sure that you are making the best possible use of the space you have already. There may be a product not worth continuing, junk stored in space which could be used for other things, or even a bad layout which, if rearranged, could satisfy your space needs. Clearly, if a way can be found to avoid taking on a new building a great deal of money will be saved. However, if you have no alternatives, then in addition to the financial demands that will arise, a number of other questions need to be answered. These questions include:

• Where will the premises be located? If an additional building is being considered, how far is it from the first building?
 If a larger building is being considered where should it be?
 Your employees' journeys to work will be affected and, in the case of having two buildings, you will have to travel between them yourself. Two buildings, unless adjacent, may also create difficulties in making optimum use of equipment – or duplicating it. How close

should new premises be to customers, sub-contractors, railway station, road depots, suppliers?

- How much additional space is needed?
  The larger the premises, the greater the cost, but what allowance should be made for further expansion at a later stage? Would it be cheaper in the long run to take a little too much space now rather than repeating the exercise after two or three years?
- What sort of premises are needed?
  Would a showroom be a good idea? How posh should the building be? What is needed in the way of parking space, inside and outside storage, waste disposal, water supply
  (Look again at your homework under 5-4)
- What local-authority restrictions may be encountered?
  Noise, smell, smoke or traffic problems may arise, depending on the nature of your business, and what may be acceptable in your present location may not be in the next

STUDY 3 – MANPOWER

What new staff will be needed? How many and with which skills?

Is there a good local supply of the type of labour needed and how long will it take to recruit and train them?

You may not need all the new staff to start at the same time. Indeed, if recruitment can be phased over a period then money will be saved and training made easier. Some careful timing may be necessary to ensure that you have neither untrained staff standing about waiting for something to do, nor machinery idle for want of an operator.

Another essential part of the planning will be arrangements to ensure that, while you are busy with all the work involved in the expansion scheme (e.g. training, finance, looking at buildings, selecting equipment), there is someone else available *and able* to look after the day-to-day running of the business. If you have no partners or employee already having sufficient know-how, then some training must be allowed as a preliminary to delegation. (What are the results of your homework in 5-9?)

STUDY 4 – EQUIPMENT

The expansion may require additional machinery, vehicles, office equipment or furniture. The opportunity should be taken to review present equipment and how it is used.

Can anything be used more efficiently? An example might be a micro-computer which, with additional or more sophisticated software, could handle additional work or simply produce results more quickly. The following questions should be answered:

- What output levels must be catered for?
- What, if any, new equipment is needed?
- Which equipment offers the best value for money?
- How well will new equipment 'match in' with the present items, i.e. are they compatible?
- Will secondhand equipment be good enough and how much expenditure would be saved?

(What conclusions did you reach from homework done for chapters 5 and 7?)

STUDY 5 – COSTING

Any decisions you have made in the preceding studies should now be costed. You may decide that, regardless of your prospects for providing or finding the necessary finance, a particular idea is not likely to be profitable, or just that your 'gut-feeling' tells you to think again. Do not hesitate to think again and again until you feel confident that your scheme is feasible in all respects.

A decision must also be made as to the size of the steps you will take. A large increase in activity implies larger funding requirements, e.g. for machines or premises, and if production goes up, so must sales effort, storage capacity and everything else.

Remember that overhead costs will go up in large chunks (e.g. the rent for a new shop or warehouse) and this changes the break-even point. The best approach is to work out the smallest steps that can be taken at a time having regard to staff and their training, reaction of competition, and so on. Getting there by three small steps is far better than falling down on one big one.

Profit calculation

When examining the alternatives (e.g. size of steps), work out a budget for each, add in a sales estimate, and produce a profit forecast. This will give you a fighting chance of choosing the best 'mix' of alternatives from a profitability angle and determining which is closest to your personal ambitions.

Developing another new business

An entirely new business, either replacing your present one or additional to it, is another option open to you. You are already only too well aware of the agonies and otherwise of starting a business, as you have done it before. However, with a business already in existence, you have an opportunity to take advantage of one or more of three alternatives, viz:

- Vertical integration
- Associated or complementary trading
- Diversification

Vertical integration involves acquiring or creating the means to do the things which either your customers do or your suppliers do. For example, a manufacturer may set up his own retail shops, or a retailer may manufacture the things he sells rather than buy them. A wholesaler may add a retail side to his business, a timber company go into forestry, or a bookseller take up publishing.

The principle is to add on to the business the activities of other businesses buying or supplying, in order to take the profits from both activities – or even three of them. An example is Boots PLC who manufacture, at Nottingham, a substantial part of their sales range. Vertical integration can also offer the advantage of more certainty of supply – if done properly.

Associated or complementary trading can also offer greater profit opportunities. An associated or complementary business is one which uses closely similar skills and other resources to the 'parent' business, e.g.

- A restaurant branching into outside catering
- A printer offering a design service
- A freight forwarder offering cargo insurance
- A garden centre doing landscape gardening

Some of these expansions to a business have some similarity to integration and there may be features of both present. Such was the case of a haulage company who used their premises to provide a vehicle-repair service. Look back, at this point, to your homework for chapter 8.

Diversification can encompass both vertical integration and complementary trading or be entirely separate.

The tobacco companies have been diversifying into a range of activities since the health scares started, including foods, alcohol and leisure. This is to give them greater security as cigarette sales fall and their income is eroded.

A further opportunity to look for and exploit is the chance to use the same resources for both businesses. The dairy companies, when selling bread as well as milk, are using the same roundsman and the same delivery vehicle and thereby saving money – or, put another way, making more income from the same resources.

Care must be taken in considering any of these opportunities to ensure that not only is the market and everything else you need there, but that you also have the commercial and management skills to handle the new element of your business. The answer might be found in buying an existing business (a subject dealt with below) or by not moving too far from familiar ground. It is one thing to add a theatre-ticket agency to a travel agency, but quite another to branch out into chartering aircraft.

Buying another business

Buying another business can be related to closing down and starting again, doing more of the same, diversifying, vertical integration or complementary trading. Buying therefore is another way to accomplish the ideas already mentioned but with the advantage that:

- an existing business will already be set up with employees, product, market, premises, equipment and, hopefully, income

Precautions when buying a business

First, confirm in your own mind from the homework you have already done what sort of business you want and where it should be. Next, line up your professional advisers, including:

- An accountant to audit and report on the books
- A valuer to report on the premises
- A solicitor to look after the contracts

These are all specialist areas requiring specialist handling. Remember that under English law the onus is on the buyer to make suitable enquiries and, short of fraud on the part of the vendor, the principle *caveat emptor* applies.

Make your intentions known to your professional advisers *before* doing anything else, as they may have good advice to offer which is applicable to the early stages of the buying process. Further particular precautions will be mentioned as we work through the buying process.

Finding the business you want

With a written description of the ideal business for your purposes you can make your needs known to people offering a 'finding' service. You might of course save yourself some fees by keeping your ear to the ground and finding a suitable business yourself, but it is likely that you will use one or more of the following:

- Your accountant, who may act for a proprietor who is about to retire, or someone else he encounters in his professional life
- Larger firms of accountants who specialize in buying and selling businesses
- Your solicitor
- Estate agents. Many have commercial departments but do not be surprised if they are not especially helpful.

Experience of estate agents is patchy – perhaps because they make so much money on house sales!

● For larger purchases, some of the merchant banks may be able to help

There are also advertisements in the press and trade magazines where you may find what you are looking for. At all events be prepared for a hard slog. Business-hunting is about as much fun as house-hunting, with the added factor that your livelihood may depend on doing it well.

Putting a value on the business offered

Unfortunately there is no nice, easy equation which can be used in valuing a business. Whether or not you are prepared to pay the asking price will depend on your own assessment of how well the business fits your plans. For example, the buildings may have a price put on them by a professional surveyor, but if they are in a poor position for your purposes then the value to you will be less. So it's to some extent a matter of reconciling value and price. Despite this rather nebulous aspect, there are a number of tangible things to be done:

● Land or property can be surveyed and reported on by your surveyor who can give an opinion as to the market value. You will in any case need a report on the condition of the premises
● Stock value must be assessed and this must be done to a formula agreed between yourself and the vendor. Stock can be valued in a variety of ways, including:
    The current price from a supplier
    The price paid to the supplier
    The price that could be obtained by selling the stock

Some variation of any of these with an allowance for insurance, freight costs, etc.

It is as important to agree which of these methods is used as it is to value the stock at all. The purchaser will have great difficulty in obtaining redress after the sale if there has been any uncertainty beforehand

- Debts outstanding should be examined to see how good (or bad) they are. Any very old debts are suspect and should be treated with caution

Loans made by the business should also be closely examined and for both debts and loans a warranty sought from the vendor that he will indemnify you should any go sour

- The books and bank statements will need to be audited by your professional representative who should be asked to comment on the cash-flow picture as well as profits

- Goodwill, the excess price above net-assets value, must be established

A common formula used to work out a price for a business is to add the net-asset value to a multiple of the profit, e.g.:

Net-asset value £100,000
Profits £25,000
Goodwill = 2 × Profits = £50,000
Price = £100,000 + £50,000 = £150,000

Obviously, if this formula is used, the multiple chosen is the important factor. This is also a point for careful negotiation with the vendor.

Other aspects of buying

Succession can be a significant factor, especially in retailing and other businesses where the personality of the proprietor may be an important feature. It is often tackled by arranging with the vendor that he will stay on for a month or two to introduce you to customers, show you some of the tricks of the trade, and generally ease the handover.

This method sometimes works well, but there is always the danger of conflict with the vendor who may not approve of your ideas, may indulge in much head-shaking in front of customers and staff, and generally hinder your inevitable 'new broom' approach. I would recommend a compromise plan involving:

- Very careful appraisal of the business before take-over
- A detailed and carefully thought-out plan of action
- An arrangement with the vendor that he will be available on a consultancy basis for a suitable period – but will not be on the premises

This arrangement will probably give you the freedom of a clean break combined with the vendor's know-how and experience.

Employees will require careful treatment, particularly as they will be apprehensive and worried about their future security and happiness. They will probably not know you and will wonder what sort of person you are to work for. They will also resist changes, albeit unconsciously.

A plan of campaign must be thought out and implemented to obtain the enthusiastic support of the staff rather than their sullen acceptance of you. This plan should include:

- Group and individual meetings with the employees to let them get to know you and you them
- Explanations of your ideas and plans and the reasons behind them

- Listening to what the employees say about your ideas and giving them every opportunity to voice their opinions. Since they have been in the business longer than you they can probably tell you many things which make a lot of sense
- Consideration for their rights, perks and benefits
- Taking things slowly at first and avoiding a great traumatic burst of new methods, rules, etc. (unless, of course, you have already found out that a quick change in some respect will positively please employees)

Keep in mind that while a human and considerate approach is definitely best, the business is yours and you must not be seen as a soft touch. Friendly, Fair and Firm is a good motto.

Franchising

Franchising is growing fast in all Western countries, and offers some definite attractions to the entrepreneur wishing to grow. The range of businesses being franchised is wide and includes hotels, fast foods, printing, car exhausts, car windscreens and driving schools.

The advantages of this method are:

- The product is normally tried, tested and well advertised
- The experience of previous franchisees can be checked to see what level of profit can be expected
- Banks and other sources of finance tend to look favourably on requests for loans for a reputable franchise

There are, of course, some disadvantages, and these can only be evaluated by a very careful study of the franchise contract. The contract will (or should) spell out the rights *and the obligations* of the franchisee, and should be thoroughly understood before any agreement is entered into. For example, you may be restricted to buying stock from the franchiser or you may have territorial or other limits imposed on you. You may find the contract terms entirely acceptable, but it is wise to be sure in advance exactly what they are.

There are solicitors with experience of franchise contracts who should be consulted; in addition, information can be obtained from the British Franchising Association, 75a Bell Street, Henley-on-Thames, Oxfordshire.

These, then, are some of the ways and means to grow, leaving us with the vital topic of financing.

Raising the money

You may, as a result of the homework done for chapter 4 (4-8), have already found all or some of the financial resources necessary for your growth plan. It is more than likely, however, that you will need to borrow money to some extent, and success in doing this depends on two factors – presenting your case and going to the best place.

Presenting your case, as you will have experienced, involves rather more than strolling into a convenient bank and asking for a million-pound loan. Banks and other lenders make their living by lending money to finance *promising* schemes where there is a real prospect of being paid back with interest. The lender needs to be convinced that your idea fits this requirement, and it is entirely reasonable that he should expect you to demonstrate it. Fortunately the banks have made it easier for us by setting out on paper the information they need and, if the questions they ask are properly answered, a good start has been made.

As an example, the National Westminster Bank, in their booklet *Presenting your case*, ask for:

A brief synopsis of your background, age, experience, etc.

Details of your business – when founded, how it has evolved
                      – reputation and accountancy system
                      – past three years' audited accounts
                      – profit and loss account
                      – borrowing history
                      – description of assets

Details of your key employees

Your purpose
                      – the plan
                      – practical aspects
                      – property details (if relevant)
                      – contingency plans
                      – relevance to existing operations

Your market
                      – estimated demand
                      – competition
                      – your competitive advantages
                      – marketing costings
                      – technology type

Your profit
                      – costings and calculations
                      – profit projections
                      – capital aspects
                      – tax, stamp duty and other costs

The amount required, when, and whether in the form of an overdraft or term loan

Your own contribution

Repayment
                      – cash-flow projections
                      – break-even point
                      – feasibility of contingency plans
                      – interest-rate effects

Security	– assets available
	– independent valuation of assets
	– agreement of other interested parties
	– insurances

You will have noticed that, if you have done all the homework in the preceding chapters, you will already have most, if not all, of the answers to these questions. Some would-be borrowers resent having to answer all these questions, regarding them as time-wasting, bureaucratic obstacles. In fact they represent information which every businessman should *in any case* have for his business in order to run it properly and, if not, the discipline of finding out the answers will improve his chances of success.

So the first requirement is a comprehensive and carefully prepared report covering the subjects listed above. It is a good idea to prepare, in addition, a one- or two-page summary and to give the whole lot to the person you will negotiate with *before* you meet. The summary will ease the burden of analyzing a lengthy document, and delivery of it in advance will give him time to read it before you turn up bursting with ideas and enthusiasm. Having read it in advance the lender may also have developed the same enthusiasm.

The next thing to decide is where to go to ask for money. Most of us think first of our bank manager, so let's deal with that possibility first.

The larger banks all offer much the same alternatives, including:

- Overdraft
  – normally used to finance working capital and to cover short-term needs

- Term loans — medium- to long-term loans with a fixed rate of interest
- Business-development loans — available for periods of 1 to 20 years at a fixed interest rate
- Small-firms loan-guarantee scheme — a scheme involving the Department of Trade and Industry who guarantee a proportion of the loan
- Franchising — Special packages for people considering some of the leading franchises

From time to time the major banks will produce new schemes or variations on the old ones, and literature is readily available.

Apart from the major high-street banks, there is a considerable range of other lenders, including companies who provide venture capital combined with an equity holding. They will, however, allow you to retain control. A few examples are listed below and, as you will see, they are often subsidiaries of the big banks:

Barclays Development Capital: owned by Barclays Bank Group

Birmingham Technology Ltd: owned by Lloyds Bank, Birmingham City Council and Aston University

Castle Finance: owned by Norwich Union Insurance

Citicorp Development Capital: owned by Citibank

Clydesdale Bank Industrial Finance: owned by Clydesdale Bank and Midland Bank

Meriton Investments: owned by Midland Bank and Rolls Royce Pension Fund

There are many more of these venture capital companies, and your accountant or bank manager should have details of them.

Another source of funds can be various government, quasi-government and local-authority bodies

If you need funding for a business in a development area you may qualify for a grant. The appropriate Regional Development Grant Office can provide up-to-date details.

Similarly, the Council for Small Industries in Rural Areas (CoSIRA) offers help to businesses employing 20 or less people in rural areas and country towns. CoSIRA, in addition to its own loan fund, has an arrangement with National Westminster Bank which facilitates larger loans for buildings and equipment. CoSIRA can be found at 141 Castle Street, Salisbury, Wiltshire, SP1 1EX.

Private investors might be interested in putting money into your business by means of the Business Expansion Scheme. The scheme, covering almost all types of business except overseas companies and financial services, offers tax relief *to the investor*, who must not be your spouse, parent or grandparent or hold a directorship. Full details of the scheme and of those who qualify to participate in it can be obtained from the Board of Inland Revenue, Somerset House, London, WC2R 1LB.

HOMEWORK – CHAPTER 19

19-1. Review your start-up experiences as a reminder of pitfalls and opportunities.

19-2. Decide whether you should expand what you are doing now, diversify, buy more premises, buy another business – or any other alternative as suggested in this chapter.

19-3. Fit your decisions into your plan and allow for all the necessary actions to be taken, such as preparing a report for the bank (or other lender), appraising a potential purchase, engaging a surveyor, etc.

19-4. Continue to keep your employees and advisers informed.

19-5. Check, re-check and check again to see that your plan is feasible and complete.

CHAPTER 20

Let's Go

You have now reached the stage where, with the results of your 'homework', you are all set to implement the plan to reach whatever objective you have decided on. In this chapter we will look at the stages of the 'battle plan'. These fall under the headings of 'preparation'; 'implementation and control'; 'revisions'; and 'follow-up'.

Preparation

A detailed plan of action is now required amounting to a timetable of action to be taken and designed to ensure that changes are implemented in the right order. For example, there is no point in arranging an interview with your bank manager until you have prepared a report for him, or in ordering machinery before you have the money to pay for it. An effective tool which will help to get things in the right order and also give you a means to check progress is an action chart, as shown in Fig. 20-1.

The chart not only records what has to be done and in what order, but also the period of time in which doing something is feasible. Smith, for example, is destined to take over branch 1, but he cannot do so until he has completed a training course. The course takes place in week 2, so he cannot start his work in branch 1 until week 3. Similarly, the clearance sale cannot start until the stock-taking is complete and, since this will take two weeks, the clearance sale cannot start until week 4.

The use of such a chart will not only help to prevent muddles but will act as a 'check-list' of things to be done.

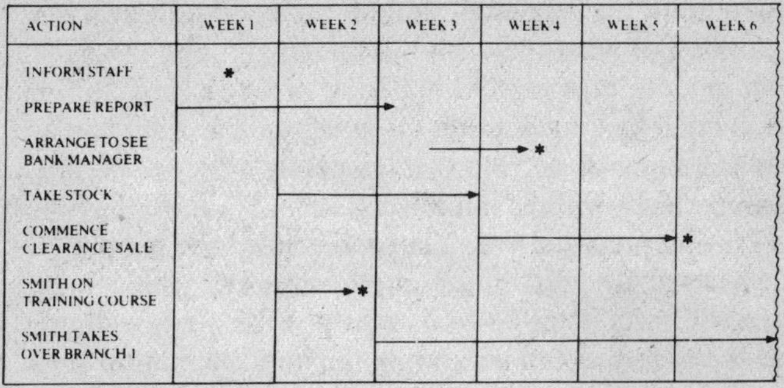

Fig. 20-1. Action chart   * = Expected completion time

Without some form of written list it is only too easy to forget something – only to be painfully reminded when things go wrong.

The action chart can include work to be done by your solicitor and other specialists and take account of mandays lost to holidays or other known absences. You may find that there is so much to be done that it is helpful to put only major headings on the action chart and to prepare additional check-lists of small items which will be 'activated' at the appropriate times. Such check-lists can be handed out to any employees involved in the scheme, thus giving them a clear idea of what you want them to do.

It is as well to build in some 'contingency time' to allow for things going wrong, such as someone going sick or a delivery not being made. Something always goes wrong at some time or another, so allowance should be made for it – a form of safety factor.

The more time and thought given to the preparation stage, the more smoothly things will go. Like a military operation, every detail should be checked, everyone informed of what they need to know, and also what they will find interesting. The people around you will be motivated by knowing what is going on and what you are doing, and can act more intelligently when a situation arises which requires initiative.

Having prepared your plan and briefed the people, the next stage of preparation is to bring everything in the present business as up to date as possible. You will need all the time you can get during the implementation stage, so it is worth burning some midnight oil to clear any outstanding correspondence, check that stocks are adequate, orders placed, instructions given, and so on. Ideally, you will have trained someone to keep things going for you while your attention is diverted elsewhere.

Implementation and control

Using your action chart you can now set in motion the first stages of the plan and, by referring to the action chart/check-list, keep an eye on whether or not things are being done on time. If something does not take place as and when it should, the action chart will enable you to see what effect the failure will have and give you a guide as to the remedial action necessary. For example, if a key action, such as exchanging contracts on a building, is delayed, then a number of other things must be re-scheduled. If this is done in a controlled way the damage is lessened or avoided.

Continue to keep people informed, especially of any changes to the timetable, so that they can make the necessary adjustments and possibly give you ideas to bring things back on target. Continue to keep your objective in mind and ensure that others, such as your accountant or solicitor, are well aware of it. They are unlikely to be working exclusively for you and the demands of their other clients can make them forget your needs or reduce priority for your work.

Revision

However good your plan, and however carefully you monitor and control your actions, you will always be exposed to circumstances beyond your control. These circumstances might include:

- Actions of a competitor
- Sudden shift in interest rates
- Someone dies, e.g. the vendor of a building you want to buy
- The council announces a new road scheme which cuts your lorry park in half
- VAT is increased
- A financial backer pulls out
- An unexpected price increase for a vital raw material

You may, of course, experience a very helpful change, such as a competitor closing down, a hefty fall in fuel-oil prices, or a tax reduction which the government introduces to encourage businesses like yours. Alternatively, you may, with experience acquired during the implementation stage, spot a golden opportunity which you had not been aware of before.

Any of these events should cause you to go back to the drawing-board to re-think what you are doing. If it is desirable, don't hesitate to revise your objective or major parts of your plan.

Don't be embarrassed to go to your financial backers or legal advisers with a revised scheme if it makes sense.

They, being professionals, should appreciate and respect your decision.

Follow-up

Having achieved your objective, you may not only have a bigger operation to handle but face the temptation to say, 'I've made it and now I can relax a little.' I'm sorry, but you can't relax, because with a bigger operation you will have a whole new set of demands made on you.

There is a huge difference between managing a business with, say, six employees and one with, say, 60 employees. In the smaller business you could always see what was going on and, indeed, would do much of the work yourself. In a larger operation you have to delegate work, and you will need a formal and more sophisticated communication and control system.

There may be, for the first time, unions to deal with, more complex storage problems, a larger element of research and development, quality-control problems, and a more complicated distribution system. The list does not end there, and you will need to learn how to handle these new challenges. This will mean reading books on management techniques or operation-research techniques. Do not scorn the need to read or the idea of taking courses on management.

Michael started a small manufacturing business at the age of 27 years, having spent some years in the RAF.

'I learned my technical skills in the RAF and this helped me to get going and build my business to a fair size in only a few years. I was doing well and was offered financial backing by an old friend who had inherited a lump sum of money. I took my time over deciding what to do and worked out the best way to make use of the opportunity. I took the plunge and bought an old vehicle-repair business and converted it into a larger version of what I had before. All went well for some time and then I began to receive complaints from customers. Deliveries were delayed and I could not see why. Quality was also a problem and replacements were costing a fortune. When customers began to leave me I became really scared and employed a consultant to tell me what was wrong.

'The consultant showed me how little I had developed my senior employees to share the management burden and how much I needed to learn about such things as quality sampling and distribution planning. I had also spent too much time dealing with routine paperwork which could have been done by a clerk and was out of touch with events on the shop floor. Because I had not developed my employees to enable them to make decisions things came to a grinding halt until I was available to sort out any problem.

'Getting myself right was the first thing I had to do, and I started with a five-day management course at Cranfield School of Management followed, a few months later, by a course at the Production Engineering Research Association at Melton Mowbray. Although I could barely afford the time these courses opened my eyes to the techniques available and since then I have never looked back. My senior employees have also attended suitable courses and this has not only made them technically more able but more motivated too.'

You may have had management training before you started your business and it is not a bad idea to drag out any old notes you had from courses in the past or refresh your memory with a good general book plus, perhaps, one or two books on specialized subjects. Your follow-up must also include a continuous review of your activities and, over and over again, all the homework you have done so far. The process never ends . . .

We have now reached the end of the book but the beginning of your more profitable future. All you need now is luck. Good luck!

Sources of Help

In addition to organizations already mentioned readers may find the following suggestions helpful.

Short training films (16mm or video) can be obtained from:
  VIDEO ARTS LIMITED
  Dumbarton House
  68 Oxford Street
  London W1N 9LA
These are the well known John Cleese films, covering a range of topics from selling technique to basic accounting principles. In addition, Video Arts produce a range of booklets which, although intended to be read in conjunction with the films, stand alone as brief and helpful explanations of the various topics.

THE BRITISH INSTITUTE OF MANAGEMENT publish a range of books, guides, check-lists and reports designed for businesses. Particularly good value are the check-lists which ask thought-provoking questions on subjects such as 'Material Handling Costs', 'Marketing Strategy' and 'Improving Office Efficiency'.

A catalogue can be obtained from PROFESSIONAL PUBLISHING LTD. Tel: 01-930 6073.

CRANFIELD SCHOOL OF MANAGEMENT can be found at Cranfield, Bedford MK43 0AL. Tel: 0234 751122. The Director of Marketing can provide details of the training course programme which, in 1986, includes:

A 5-day course on Finance and Accounting
A 5-day course on Marketing
A 2-day seminar on improving sales performance
A 3-day course on preparing marketing plans
A 4-day course on Industrial Relations.

For those who can spare the time, Cranfield offer courses up to 6 weeks in duration covering management in some depth.

Details of training courses at about 150 other colleges and institutions around the country can be obtained from *Management Training Directory*, published by Alan Armstrong & Associates Ltd, 72 Park Road, London NW1 4SH.

For those who wish to obtain a working knowledge of tax systems, the *Daily Mail Income Tax Guide* is an inexpensive starting point. In addition to personal taxation the guide also covers such matters as capital allowances, company cars, corporation tax and partnership tax.

A good book on organization and methods is worth reading by any businessman at any time. Unfortunately the subject is out of fashion and you may have to scour the shelves of second-hand bookshops. Look out for *Organization and Methods* by A. G. Anderson (MacDonald and Evans Ltd). This book, although badly laid-out and cramped, is full of ideas and teaches the O & M approach – a useful skill for anyone in business.

Finally, a worthwhile book which advocates simple but effective methods is *Practical Corporate Planning* by John Argenti, available in paperback from Allen and Unwin. Argenti gives helpful advice on setting objectives, forecasting (and dealing with the errors in forecasts), looking at trends and alternative strategies. All very clear and it makes the reader think.

Good reading (and viewing)!

Index

Sports and activities handbooks now available in Panther Books

Pat Davis Badminton Complete (illustrated)	£1.25	☐
Bruce Tegner Karate (illustrated)	£1.50	☐
Bruce Tulloh The Complete Distance Runner (illustrated)	£1.95	☐
Meda Mander How to Trace Your Ancestors (illustrated)	£1.50	☐
Tom Hopkins How to Master the Art of Selling	£2.50	☐
William Prentice How to Start a Successful Business	£2.50	☐
Susan Glascock A Woman's Guide to Starting Her Own Business	£2.50	☐
Alfred Tack Sell Your Way to Success	£1.25	☐
Andrew Pennycook The Book of Card Games	£3.95	☐
C Lukács and E Tarjan Mathematical Games	£1.50	☐
Gyles Brandreth The Complete Puzzler	£1.50	☐
Patrick Duncan (ed.) The Panther Crossword Compendium (Vols 1 and 2)	£1.95 each	☐
Quizwords 1	£1.50	☐
Quizwords 2	£1.50	☐

To order direct from the publisher just tick the titles you want
and fill in the order form.

HB1081

All these books are available at your local bookshop or newsagent, or can be ordered direct from the publisher.

To order direct from the publishers just tick the titles you want and fill in the form below.

Name _____

Address _____

_____

Send to:
Grafton Cash Sales
PO Box 11, Falmouth, Cornwall TR10 9EN.

Please enclose remittance to the value of the cover price plus:

UK 55p for the first book, 22p for the second book plus 14p per copy for each additional book ordered to a maximum charge of £1.75.

BFPO and Eire 55p for the first book, 22p for the second book plus 14p per copy for the next 7 books, thereafter 8p per book.

Overseas £1.25 for the first book and 31p for each additional book.

Grafton Books reserve the right to show new retail prices on covers, which may differ from those previously advertised in the text or elsewhere.